FINANCIAL

M000119504

earn
grow
give

Simple Steps to Grow Your Money
While Creating a Rich Life

INSPIRATION, IDEAS AND STRATEGIES TO INCREASE
YOUR CASH FLOW AND GROW YOUR MONEY WHILE
LIVING A LIFE OF PURPOSE AND ABUNDANCE

CAMILLE GAINES
CEO of Financial Woman

Camille Gaines Publishing
ISBN-10: 061552026X
ISBN-13: 978-0615520261

Additional copies of this book are available at www.FinancialWoman.com.

Presented by Financial Woman
3801 N Capital of Texas Hwy, Ste E240-452
Austin, TX 78746 USA
866-858-9023

*This book is dedicated in loving memory
to my father, Richard Allen Robinson, who
taught me the principles of both investing
and life with his wisdom*

*To my mother, Maxine Robinson, who
continues to model strength, excellence,
and giving so beautifully*

TABLE OF CONTENTS

PART TWO

STEPS YOU MUST TAKE FOR GROWING YOUR MONEY

ABOUT THE AUTHOR

Camille Gaines is a leader in helping women gain financial independence. She resonates with those who are trying to begin saving money each month while living a quality life, are ready to begin investing, or have accumulated wealth that deserves more attention, because Camille has been in that exact same place at some point on her own money journey. She shares simple and practical solutions in everyday language so that others can gain from her experience to enhance their financial destiny.

Camille's goal is that of building a company that inspires every woman to embrace her own financial journey. "Knowledge is what brings financial security" Camille explains. "This is a huge insight for many women who are too busy to be proactively involved with their finances or default to the unconscious belief that a man will take care of them".

Camille is the founder and CEO of FinanicalWoman. com, host of Financial Woman Radio, and has an award winning blog. What sets her apart from many others offering financial education is that she is on the investor side of the table herself, not selling wealth management products or advisory services; this allows her to be completely unbiased and present various options based on personal experience so that a woman can wisely choose what will give her financial freedom.

Camille's passion for investing began when she saw her father successfully time the purchase of tax free municipal bonds selling at deep discounts in the early 1980's. Those bonds greatly appreciated and paid tax free interest up to 20% over the next decade, allowing her father to take an early retirement and enhancing her parent's lifestyle.

Following those early lessons, Camille loves finding value everywhere, from undervalued securities to designer jewellery online. While many may avoid financial topics, Camille asks what cannot be fun about giving your money attention when it provides so much, including food and shelter; it gives you the ability to change your life and even the lives of others. Camille would love to share what she has learned about money and investing to help you create the rich life that you desire.

Connect with Camille at:

Website: http://www.FinancialWoman.com
Twitter: http://twitter.com/camillegaines
Facebook: http://www.facebook.com/financialwoman

A FEW ACKNOWLEDGEMENTS

Thank you to Bunny, Rennie, and Shelby for helping me with editing and producing this book, to the Financial Woman team, especially Gerda and Kathy for always having my back, to my business coach, Sheri McConnell for inspiring and challenging me to grow, to Sandra Yancey, Founder and CEO, eWomenNetwork, Inc. for giving me a chance from the get-go, and to my friends, Denise Flint, Lorin Beller Blake, Marie Snidow, Kathy Wiggin, Molly McNichols, Rebecca Cohen, Catherine Mize and Sara Ragsdale for supporting and encouraging me.

Thank you to my teachers at Joyner Elementary School in Tupelo, Missisippi, especially Mrs.Wiggins, who told me I was a good writer, Mrs. Cheney, who told me I was artistic, and Mrs. Carroll, who told me I could perform. I don't know if I could do any of those things, but at the time, I believed them, and I still remember! To Cecelia

Fleishhacker, my Girl Scout leader, who taught me that different is not only ok, it's good.

Thank you to the wonderful leaders who have inspired me to grow through your speeches, books, programs and media presentations; your quotes are found throughout this book. Many of you don't know me, but I feel like I know you, because you have touched upon my life in a meaningful way.

Thank you, especially to my husband, Larry, for supporting my goals and always valuing my input, and to Lawrence and Cameron, for both encouraging and challenging me to grow.

Thank you to my parents, Richard Allen and Maxine Robinson, and my "big" brother, Blake, for all you have taught me from your fine examples, and for always being there for me.

INTRODUCTION

I thought for certain there was something wrong with me. I treasured being with my children during the years I stayed home to raise them, but I have always needed some form of serious mental stimulation to be happy. To fulfil this need, I spent much time enjoying financial books, taking courses, and researching stocks, bonds and mutual funds to learn about personal investing during the time I left my career to live overseas with my husband. My quest for knowledge was based on my love of financial information, as much as my drive to continue to be a smart and capable woman who could land on two feet, regardless of what life dealt me. The problem was that I had no one with whom I could share this passion, especially living on an island as an ex-patriot spouse, pre-internet, for the most part. Although I was in the company of some amazing women from all over the world, the conversations at playgroups and golf games were just not about the yield spread between municipals and treasuries or the S&P 500. When my husband came home from trading securities for one of the world's largest private energy trading companies in the world each day, he wasn't really interested in discussing financial matters with me.

I felt alone and different, yet, I continued to pursue my passion. The challenges in our lives often lead to rewarding results. Out of this experience, I created a business to connect women who want to embrace their financial health so that they don't have to be alone in their quest to become smart and proactive about their money. It is sheer a pleasure for me to now be sharing the information that I have learned over the past thirty years from my education, a career, and as both a personal investor and business owner. I so enjoy giving courses and coaching women to create a rich life! The timing was perfect, because, more than ever, women are embracing their own financial wellness, and they can now easily be part of a supportive group of other like-minded women through FinancialWoman.com.

The Past Four Years

If you are going to write a book, write quickly, because as you grow and change, what you want to say changes. Who you are, and how you think changes, based on new experiences and new information. During the almost four year period that I have been writing this book, I dramatically changed what I wanted to share in its contents. My life has changed, as do most lives over four years, but I have found that some periods bring more change than others. My children became young adults, my home suddenly became much larger than it needed to be, and I fulfilled a dream: I created my very own business around a passion. I have gone from being too insecure to even say that I teach women about the often "taboo" topic of money and investing, to not being able to shut up about it! I found more and more that I wanted to share from my own life and expansive financial journey that I thought would help other women on theirs. Now I am also passionate about helping other women "come out of the closet" with their talents and knowledge, in whatever area it lies, so that they, too, can earn, grow and give. It's more fun than you can imagine!

In addition to all of these personal developments, the largest financial crisis since 1929 occurred, for heaven's sake. How can that not change the attitude and experiences of someone who not only personally invests, but also teaches others about investing? I still want to provide unbiased information to help you confidently make informed decisions about your money. For example, I want to share with you that the economy moves in somewhat logical cycles that affect the value of your investments; I want to teach you a simple tool that allows you to easily build a diversified portfolio or evaluate the performance of any investment you own or money manager you use. And I still want to share why the value of long term bonds decreases when interest rates go up, so you understand that the safety of bonds can be a misperception. There is so much more of this type of information I want to share so that you can feel more in control of your money. I have shared (snuck?) some of this information in this book, but I also felt a strong urge to share why, as a woman, it's time for you to embrace your financial journey, if you are not already doing so. Embrace all aspects of that journey; your power to earn (whether from your investment capital or your skills), grow (both your money and your abilities), and then give (your time, your talents and your money) to change lives; your life, the life of your family, and the lives of others. This book begins with clarifying the reasons why your money matters, because this is the starting point in giving your money the attention that it deserves. This book became about creating the life that you want to create: a rich life.

How This Came To Be

My parents grew up during the Great Depression. This fact affected the lives of my brother, Blake, and me, as it did so many others in the baby boomer generation. My mother was one of eleven children in a family that lived on a farm in Arkansas. She was the first woman in her family to graduate from high school. (There were 4 older sisters.) The school required a long walk on many dark and cold mornings along the isolated train tracks. She walked to school, anyway. She knew that she wanted to create a rich life for herself; she wanted to develop her talents. She wanted to learn new skills so that she could be financially independent, instead of simply living a life that was the norm, and thus, expected of her: to marry a farmer, and live the rest of her life in a tiny town (with less than 500 residents). It's not that this would have been a bad life, but it wasn't the life that she chose for herself. She devised a plan, as a teenager, to create the life that she wanted. She borrowed $50 from Uncle Vernon so that she could take the bus to Memphis to get a job; and that she did. She then learned that she was an excellent typist, a skill that was highly in demand in the 1940's. She found a room in a boarding house, where she lived and supported herself for several years.

Eventually, she met and married my dad. They began researching and investing in the stock market, as soon as they had the funds to do so. Later, as a stay at home mom, she ran our household like a little business, putting aside as much money as she could, to grow. For example, she wanted a new set of furniture for my bedroom, so she ordered a kit and built a beautiful set of furniture that she "antiqued" off-white. (Can you even imagine researching this from a small town, without the internet?)

The furniture was only one of many projects that required our living room to become a workshop for various projects that my mother passionately pursued to provide an excellent quality of life, while staying within my parents spending plan. (You'll learn that I prefer this term over the "b word": "budget".) Mama had discovered that by ordering kits and building things herself, she could provide quality non-essentials for our family at a fraction of the cost. This allowed my parents to put aside more money to grow. She wanted to have the funds so that I could go to college one day, and have ballet, art and piano lessons in the meantime. She defined and created the life that she wanted for her family.

My mother created a little sewing business making the beautiful, detailed costumes required for numerous students in the annual dance recital. Once again, our living room was turned into a "hands off" workshop every April from the time I was 5, until I was 17. Our home was filled with lovely sequins, fabrics and netting for tutus of all colors. Sometimes, I even got to help her glue some of the multitude of sequins that couldn't be sewn. I now realize that Mama enjoyed earning "her own money" by using her talents and abilities. She thrived on sharing her gifts through that little enterprise with the creation of all of those beautiful costumes.

The largest crime my mom committed was requiring me to wear my black patent Mary Janes year round, instead of providing me with white shoes for the summer months. I still recall feeling as though I was the only girl in the entire universe without white shoes, completely oblivious to the fact that there were millions of little girls all over the world who would have given anything for a pair of shoes, especially a pair of black patent Mary Janes. What I learned from that horrible injustice is that black patent shoes are appropriate year round. (This turned out to be a very valuable lesson as an adult with my long, skinny feet that look like surf boards in white shoes!) If only I had known, then, the wise lessons my mother was providing that would serve me well for life that went well beyond shoe style.

In the meantime, my dad read the Wall Street Journal every night. He worked from 7:00 a.m. to 5:00 p.m., Monday through Friday, and from 7:00 a.m. to noon on Saturday, and every Sunday, after church, he went to check the bananas. During his lunch hour he went to the library and read Barron's. Every Tuesday night, we went to the library as a family. One year, we were featured on the local television station as the "Library Family of the Week". (Is there any way that I could NOT love creating and writing financial courses and books with this childhood and these genes?) Daddy's dream was to be a stock analyst on Wall Street, but he was the produce manager for a large food distribution company in Tupelo, Mississippi, because it supported our family. Pursuing and developing a career based on your passions was, unfortunately, not a popular concept in the 1940's. This career, however, also gave him time to fish, frequently take us out on our boat, and later become a serious golfer. His attention to investing, along with my mother's savvy cash flow abilities, allowed him to take an early retirement when the company for which he worked, for several decades, was subsequently sold. My parents began playing golf, and even built a house right on the golf course so they could have the convenience of driving onto the course in their cart from the garage. I was blessed with seeing the positive results of their financial planning all my life. And they did it all themselves, by simply deciding what they wanted, paying attention to their money and acting in ways to create the life they chose.

Both of my parents gave their time, talents and financial resources to charities throughout my entire life.

In his later years, my dad was part of a program that taught adults to read. His last client, before developing brain cancer, was a banker that had never learned to read. I still recall the absolute joy that this gave my father. He served at our church in various ways over the years. My mother still volunteers several times a month, including food distribution to those in need for three exhausting hours at a time. She has only recently stopped delivering for Meals on Wheels.

Why am I writing about my childhood and my parents? In this book, you'll read about exploring how your childhood affects your money habits, in both positive and negative ways. I wanted to share about my childhood because my parents taught me about financial responsibility through their actions. (If you were taught something different, you can change your patterns!) They also taught me about independence, diligence, and God. They taught me about creating a rich life through earning, growing and giving. It's not about getting the white shoes every spring. It's about so much more. Whatever age you are now, choose the life you want to live. Create a plan to get it, and then follow the steps to make it happen. It's your life; now go live it.

PART ONE

KEY STEPS FOR IDENTIFYING AND CREATING THE LIFE YOU WANT

CHAPTER ONE

KNOW YOUR
MONEY REASONS

You have to regain control of your thoughts, your images, your dreams and daydreams, and your behavior. Everything you think, say, and do needs to become intentional and aligned with your purpose, your values, and your goals.

— Jack Canfield

It's not about the money! You've heard it before, but what does it mean? We all know that money makes the world go 'round. It pays for nice things and provides food and shelter. It pays for family vacations, education, entertainment and diamonds; it pays for adoptions, health care and homes. Money buys those beautiful hardwood floors, that shiny new car, and those to-die-for black boots. Money provides funds for businesses, religious organizations, and charitable giving; it can make a huge difference in your life or in the life of someone else. Money can make a difference in the world, but only you know why it matters to you; only you know the changes that you want to make with your money. Nail those reasons, and you have got the foundation for managing your money well. It's called the vision for your life, a rich

RICH HABITS

Knowing your money reasons will motivate you to give your wealth the attention it deserves. This step is about much more than money; it's about having the ability to create the life you want to live.

life. It's not about money; it's about your life and your goals. It's what you want that money can buy, which, as you know, is not everything, but it is an awful lot. These are your money reasons.

The first step leading to a rich life is a simple but profound one: Decide the reasons why you want to have money. Remember that it is not money itself that enhances your quality of life, but, rather, what you can do with that money. Which of the things in the above paragraph resonated with you? There are millions of other items that could be on the list of what money can provide; the list is infinite, but your list should be all yours.

Perhaps right now you want to establish a plan to build a nest egg so you can feel more in control of your money and your life. Maybe what you really want is to be more knowledgeable and capable with your finances, so that you can feel financially independent. Or maybe what you really want more than anything is to be out of a terrible financial situation, so that you can sleep well at night and feel financially secure. If this is where you currently find yourself, what got you to this place? What did you want or think you wanted that led you to a place of so much stress and unease? Maybe your life has included some unusually hard circumstances that contributed to financial disaster. Own your part in the making of this situation, and ask what you have learned from this painful lesson. Think about what is really important to you now. Give some serious thought to the life you really want to create, so that you can know just what you want your money to do for you moving forward, wherever you may be on your financial journey.

It's All About You!

Invite the life that you want to create with this simple but powerful exercise. Set aside fifteen minutes of quiet time. Use a timer so that you'll stay completely focused. Write out your very own money reasons. Think of your reasons, not someone else's, or what you think they should be. So often we go through life thinking that we know what we want. Sometimes we live our lives based on decisions we made twenty years prior that are no longer valid, or we continue living in default mode. We work ridiculously hard and do everything in our power to get those things that we thought we wanted, only to realize that, after getting them, they were not our dreams at all, but the dreams of someone else. Perhaps they were our parent's dreams or society's dreams but not our own. What are your dreams? Have you ever sat down to really think about it? When was the last time that you did? I encourage you to think about it now. What do you really want?

Experiences or Things?

As you go through this thought process, think about whether it is the experiences that you most value or the "things" in your life. Is it the memory of that sailing vacation several years ago with your family or friends that really brings you joy, or driving your brand new car? Is it the amazing feeling of accomplishment that you get when you write a check to your favourite charity, or send your grandchild to college? Is it simply the knowledge that you can support yourself financially? There is no right or wrong answer, no guilt or judgment. We all have different wants and desires; your reasons are okay, whatever they are. Your money reasons will change as your life changes and your priorities shift. This is why it's important to rethink your money reasons at least annually.

This simple process can take as little as fifteen minutes, but be completely life changing. Maybe, when you stop to really think about it, you don't actually want that big house that keeps you financially strapped, the SUV that costs too much to fill with gas, or that vacation home, which causes a constant but unending flow of anxiety because spending time there is just one more thing to do. Or, maybe, it's the opposite. Perhaps a vacation home in the middle of the country would bring your grown family together, and you could purchase it by having a smaller primary residence. Maybe you realize that you really don't want to collect antique bunnies or fine wines anymore; you may ask yourself if you even want any more stuff. Maybe you realize that what you really want is to leave your current salaried job and build a business around a life-long desire to teach college, paint or finally develop that new product you have wanted to create for years. Maybe this thought fuels a deep desire to spend your days doing something that is in your heart instead of something that just pays all those bills. Perhaps you no longer want to grow someone else's company, or spend your precious time on an unpleasant commute. The commonality in all of this is money. Every one of these scenarios involves money, maybe less or maybe more, but it all involves that commodity we call "money."

Who Are You?

Take a good look at all areas of your life. Who are you in regard to your presence, your being and your style? Does it reflect who you are and the life you want to create? Who do you want to be? Maybe you are not about expensive platinum and diamonds, as you previously thought, but you discover that you are really turquoise and silver. Maybe you are not Jimmy Choo®, but you're vintage. Or maybe it's the other way around. Maybe you have been trying to be Timex® but you're Rolex®. (No one says that Rolex cannot come from eBay®!) These are all okay; one costs more and one costs less, but neither is right nor wrong. Define who you want to be: your style, your life, your dreams, and your goals; define what matters to you.

Examine your entire lifestyle: the car, the clothes, the jewellery, the boat, the career, the hobbies, the home and especially the job. Revisit it all because maybe the mindset that made those choices years ago is no longer valid, and maybe your precious time and money are supporting only habits that no longer reflect who you are and the life you truly desire. Your current financial situation is a reflection of the life you have created thus far.

By defining your true wants and desires, you'll be able to clarify how much money you need to create the life you now dream of having. It might be less than you thought you needed, or it might be more. If it's less, then you have discovered that you are in the blissful place of having "extra" money. If it's more money you need, as is usually the case, then you can design a plan to create the life you want. The driving force for your earning and spending habits will be getting the life you want (a pretty good motivator, when you consider that the alternative is having a life that you don't want). This is your life you are considering here. You can then make sure you are spending your money on things that are aligned with the vision that you have for your life. Your daily money habits become congruent with your vision. That is true financial peace. This will be the foundation for your commitment to earning, and then growing, your money.

Enjoy the Journey

While it's important to know what you want, it's equally important to enjoy the journey. You may be wondering how you can enjoy the journey, as all of this may feel like a life that you will enjoy at some future date. You can enjoy each and every day by focusing on what you do have. Here is my suggestion: Every morning give thanks for the abundance in your life, and every evening write five things from the day for which you feel gratitude. This only takes one or two minutes a day and is certain to make a meaningful difference in your life. Maybe the appreciation you express is as simple as the food on your table for three meals that day or a one minute connection with your challenging teen. Perhaps it is a simple insight or even a painful life lesson. Sometimes the blessing may be that you found something that you really needed at half the usual price. Seek and appreciate the abundance in your life each day to ensure that you fully embrace your life journey.

Begin a Wealth Journal

Keep your very own money reasons in front of you each day. Start a wealth journal as you begin this book and make notes on your own financial journey, both in your journal and the book. As you get ideas, highlight them and make a list of action items in your journal as you read the chapters. Begin your wealth journal entries with the reasons why you want money. Become comfortable with owning and using a wealth journal. Using the word "wealth" may feel awkward at first, but let's change that. Wealth is about so much more than a sum of money.

Summary

Knowing your life goals will motivate you to take the steps to create and reach your financial goals. After you have clearly defined your money reasons, then you'll be motivated to take the steps to get you there. You'll be living a purposeful life that is reflected in all areas, including your finances. Keep those reasons in front of you by reviewing them often. They'll lead you to a life that is truly rich.

Just for Couples

If you are in a committed relationship, or considering one, complete this money reason process together since you'll be working as a team toward the life that you want to create. Allow time for each of you to individually write out what you really want. At the end of the time, share your goals with each other, with the rule that neither of you can interrupt nor discredit the other's ideas. Just this simple exercise may expose things that you didn't know about the other; things that are really important.

You may see commonalities in your vision. For example, one of you may have written of dreaming of owning a lake house for fishing, and the other may have written of wanting a mountain vacation home for family time. The two of you can work toward a common goal, such as a second home in the mountains on or near a lake.

After you identify and understand what you each really want in life, you'll be much more likely to work together to create it. Once you begin estimating the cost of your dreams, then you can refine and blend your choices, leading to a logical

continued...

and obtainable option. This is a wonderful bonding exercise for a couple on so many levels, both practical and emotional. Besides being fun, it fuels the drive to create the life of your dreams.[1]

---

1 Inspiration for this exercise came from:
Miller, J. Keith. What to Do with the Rest of Your Life. New York. Crossroad Publishing Company, 2005

LIFE STORY

Maria was always worried about money. She had a successful career, but she felt driven to work longer hours, including Saturday's, so that she could make additional income. She missed the time away from her family. Once she took the time to write out her own money reasons, she saw that, based on the investment capital that she had already saved and a conservative estimation of her future earnings, she would be able to get the things that were most important in her life. She saw that she could reduce her work hours and start spending more time with her family. She finally felt at peace when she worked fewer hours, and she began enjoying her life more.

Financial Woman Steps

Find a quiet time and place.

Define what a rich life means to you.

Dig deep and think about what you really want.

CHAPTER TWO

RELEASE INVALID MONEY BELIEFS

Let go of who you are supposed to be and be who you are.

— **Brené Brown, PhD, LMSW**
Women and Parenting Expert

Once you have decided on your money reasons, you'll want to make sure you have the right mindset to help create the life you want. You may have childhood beliefs that affect your money habits and the way you handle the responsibilities involved with your money. These beliefs can be so deep in your subconscious mind that you have no awareness of them, but they can sabotage your efforts to be the person you want to be regarding your money. I see people allow old and invalid money beliefs to control their actions in a way that keeps them stuck in negative habits around their money. I truly believe that there is something to this element of financial conditioning that must be addressed first in most people.

Early negative experiences can also work the other way; I have seen individuals driven to remarkable success as a result of unfortunate childhood financial situations.

RICH HABITS

Create your own financial journey based on what you really believe to be true about money, not someone else's beliefs that don't serve you well.

Children, who experienced devastating chaos or significant loss, sometimes are completely driven to success because of these early life challenges. They know that they want to live a different life and provide a better life for their family, and this force can be unstoppable. If you stop and think about it, you probably know someone who fits this bill.

Negative money mindsets can also be the result of an experience that happened earlier in life but beyond childhood. Again, the outcome can lead to a positive or a negative result. Maybe you saw that those people in your community, who owned their own business, were more successful than those who didn't, or vice versa. This may have led you to a positive choice about your career. Many have experienced financing that first car loan at a high interest rate, and then the subsequent feeling of it taking an entire lifetime just to pay off the debt. The result of avoiding high interest debt, then, is a positive effect due to a negative experience. These are all examples of how money experiences can have a positive effect on subsequent money habits.

On the other hand, if you suddenly lost your first significant job, you may always be fearful that it will happen again; this may lead you to find it difficult to feel financially secure. Maybe you decided to put all of your savings into a hot stock tip that you got at a cocktail party only to see that stock lose 80% of its value within three months. As a result, it may be difficult for you to ever invest in the stock market again. This fear can remain, even though you know that you can invest in the stock market in a more logical way. For example, you can buy into a diversified fund, a method with much less risk than buying one stock. You could limit your risk even more with other strategies.

Are Your Money Habits Sabotaging You?

Early financial conditioning that is negative often leads to money habits that take us away from our goals, rather than toward them. Some of the more common habits that I see in working with women are:

- Settling for work that requires less than your best
- Avoiding involvement with your finances
- Avoidance of investing money
- A constant feeling that the bottom will drop out
- Never being able to feel financially secure
- Overspending
- Buying things you don't need
- Using high credit card debt to fund unnecessary purchases

- Believing that a man will take care of you financially

- Feeling as though your money is not your responsibility

- Avoiding debt at all costs

- Undercharging for your services or career

- Working for free

- Financial chaos

These are just a few of the many ways that negative money conditioning can manifest. Are any of these issues present in your life? Recognizing patterns that have negative financial consequences is the first step towards changing them.

Childhood Money Beliefs

The root of both good and bad financial habits is usually our past. Take a few minutes to reflect on this area. What were the beliefs, spoken or not, in your childhood home about money? As you think about this and read through the following list of questions, note in your wealth journal any feelings that arise for you around a particular question. Here are a few possibilities from among the many that we explore in one of my programs:

- Were you discouraged from certain career choices?

- Was there arguing about money or was it a source of stress?

- Did you always feel like there wasn't enough money?

- Was it always boom or bust?

- Was it bad to talk about money?

- Was it assumed or spoken that women should not be involved with the money?

- Was borrowing money bad at all costs?

- Was someone else supposed to take care of you?

- Were you encouraged to share?

- Were you encouraged to take responsibility for your money?

- Were you allowed to make decisions about your money?

- Did you receive an allowance?

Evidence suggests that these subconscious and dated beliefs contribute to our own money habits throughout our lives until we recognize them and create our own beliefs. Studies have shown repeatedly that those who win the lottery lose all the money they won within a few years. They do not believe deep down that they are deserving of wealth, or they see themselves as poor. They continue to have unhealthy money habits even after they have become wealthy. Their habits lead them back to their core beliefs.

Summary

What is your mindset when considering money? Just like with exercise, diet and relationships, you must first get your head right around your money so that you can establish and maintain good habits to earn and grow it. It is our actions that lead us to accomplishing, or not, our goals, and actions are just habits. Decide which money beliefs are holding you back, so that you can let go of debilitating habits and create good money habits that will lead you to the financial life that you choose.

 *Financial Woman Extra*

Visit **FinancialWoman.com/tools**
to download a list of affirmations to help you
with your money mindset.

LIFE STORY

Beverly owned a physical therapy business. While she had a full practice, she made enough income to just cover the bills. She began her practice to help others, so she felt it wasn't right to charge the rates that other therapists with similar experience were charging. She also frequently spent extra time with clients at the end of the sessions. Upon examining her childhood beliefs, she discovered that deep down she felt that a woman should not make more money than her husband. Once she realized this dated belief was behind her unsuccessful practice, she began charging market rates. She was also able to see more clients because she kept to her schedule. Once she developed new habits, she increased her income significantly. She then decided to spend half a day as a volunteer at a clinic providing her physical therapy services to under-privileged children. Her life became much richer once she released the false beliefs that kept her acting in ways that made her business unsuccessful.

Financial Woman Steps

What were the childhood beliefs about money in your life?

What experiences beyond childhood affected your beliefs about money?

Have these beliefs affected your money habits in a positive or negative way?

CHAPTER THREE

KNOW HOW MUCH MONEY YOU HAVE

We can't become what we need to be by remaining what we are.

— Oprah Winfrey

Every woman should know how much money she has. If you have not been tracking your net worth, it is time to start. If you wanted to buy a ticket to Paris, you would first have to know where you would be beginning your journey. Your financial journey is no different; you first have to know just where you are to get where you want to be. If you happen to work with a financial advisor or your spouse manages your money, this is no reason not to know how much money you have. It does, however, make knowing easier to avoid, and it can allow you to assume that it is someone else's responsibility.

A friend of mine had been looking for a home for some time. She mentioned that they had found one that they really liked, and her husband was meeting with their Certified Public Accountant (CPA) to figure out if they could afford the home. What? Did I hear that correctly? How could you need to ask your CPA if you can afford a

RICH HABITS

Many people go to great lengths to avoid calculating their net worth. If you are sidestepping this crucial step, look at your money mindset to see if there is something bigger that you need to address.

home? While there are some simple tax benefits to home ownership that could be helpful in the analysis, should the CPA be the one to make this call? What if the CPA has different disciplines than my friend? (Don't most CPAs?) My friend and her husband were the ones who would have to live with their decision, sign the mortgage, and live out their spending pattern to support their house payments, not the CPA. Even if the CPA did need to be a part of this decision, why wasn't my friend present at this important meeting? If you know your money reasons, your monthly cash flow and your net worth, you can figure out almost everything you need to know in order to manage your personal finances, including the amount of money to sensibly spend on a home. While you may choose to get some help in establishing a basic plan, be sure that this does not lead to avoidance of responsibility for decisions. Owning responsibility in your financial decisions will support you in accomplishing your money goals through your daily actions.

Where Are You?

Many people go to great lengths to avoid knowing just how much money they have, which is simply calculating their net worth. If you avoid knowing, something bigger is going on. It could be that you are afraid to be in charge of your money, or maybe you feel that by looking at it you know you will need to take the next step toward growing or investing it. Perhaps you know that your net worth has declined, and it feels better to avoid it rather than deal with it. Maybe you have some childhood beliefs that are no longer valid but are still controlling your money habits. See what those little voices have to say, discredit them, and then do what you need to do: calculate your net worth at least twice each year.

The best way to do this is to create a simple Own and Owe Statement. Here is what you'll need for this simple but revealing undertaking:

- Pencils and Paper (if you prefer writing)

- Spreadsheet software (if you prefer using your computer)

- Paper or Online Access for the following:
  - Account Statements, including bank statements, brokerage accounts, retirement accounts, IRAs, etc.
  - Mortgage balance
  - Value of your home if you are a homeowner
  - Credit card bills

Begin with the "Own" portion of your statement. List all of your investments from the various accounts, along with other major assets, and then total the two numbers. Next, calculate the "Owe" portion of your statement; simply list everything that you owe, or your liabilities, and total them. The difference between what you own and what you owe is your financial net worth.

Keep a copy of this statement handy and look at it monthly to help you keep an awareness of your financial big picture. If you have a private home office, a white board is an excellent place for a summary of your Own and Owe Statement. It is in your face each day, reminding you to spend wisely, invest well, and move toward your money goals. You can put a large piece of paper over it when you have visitors in your office space.

If you work with an advisor, she may already do this calculation for you, and, while her data may include assets that are outside of her oversight, it may not. If it doesn't, or if you don't work with an advisor or financial planner, create your own statement. In fact, I encourage everyone to prepare their own statement because getting "in the trenches" with your numbers increases your comfort level in working with them. Involvement also improves financial accountability.

These figures provide the foundation for your financial empowerment. There are several reasons why this simple document is important.

It allows you to easily know exactly what you have.

You may have a good idea of what your assets are off of

the top of your head, but it is easy to forget about an IRA that has outsourced management that you have no plans to change or that piece of real estate you inherited ten years ago from your grandmother. Women have shared with me that they have actually forgotten about retirement money that they had stashed away!

It provides a place to organize household assets.

If you happen to be married, this simple statement will allow you to easily see all your different accounts in one place. This becomes especially helpful for couples with multiple retirement accounts between the two of them. Several women have shared that they feel overwhelmed by the thought of tracking all the various accounts, including IRA's, college savings and regular accounts. Creating and using an Own and Owe Statement will turn the feeling of being overwhelmed into one of clarity.

It is a tool for strategizing.

Your Own and Owe Statement will provide an excellent tool for easily assessing where you are right now and what needs to be changed. It will allow you to easily track the annual changes in your investment capital from both cash flow results and investment returns. One of the most important decisions about how to grow your money will be to decide the investment objective, or outcome, you want from each account. This valuable, yet simple tool will help you easily see what money you need to focus on growing, money that may be available to generate income, and amounts to set aside for other purposes, such as college or contingencies. Additionally, you will be able to easily see which debt needs to be paid first, should you have debt with high interest rates.

Moving Forward

If you are pleased with the value of your financial net worth, then you can celebrate your good choices and plan the steps to continue your progress. If not, this is the perfect time to look at making changes, but you can't take this step until you know exactly where you are now. Note that if you are unhappy with your current net worth, you have probably learned a lot from your mistakes. It is unlikely you will make the same mistakes again, and you are now moving forward.

Try to detach your emotions from this exercise by thinking of it like a business. The business is putting your money to work for you, so that you can create a rich life. Look at where you are now, and be forward in your thinking. Learn from past mistakes, but don't let them keep you stuck in a place where you don't want to be. The main point is to track exactly where you are financially, so that you can create a plan to get where you want to be.

Summary

If you already track your net worth regularly, then you are already taking an important step toward your financial goals. If you don't, now is the time to begin. You may realize you can achieve some of your "money reasons" sooner than you thought when you calculate where you are right now in your money journey. Begin living the financial life that will lead you straight to what you really want in all areas of your life.

LIFE STORY

Sarah suddenly and unexpectedly found out that her job was being eliminated. For years, she had wanted to start her own business built around her passion for advertising, which she was able to develop in her salaried position. She had been procrastinating setting aside money to fund the business, and lived month to month from her salary. Now, she finally had the time to start her own business, and even had several potential large clients, but she lacked the financial resources to fund the initial start-up and cover her living expenses. She went through a couple of very stressful weeks and sleepless nights during the final days of her job. She was searching for new work without any luck. When she was right at the end of her employment, she learned that she had a retirement plan that she had not monitored and, subsequently, forgotten. After considering the tax consequences, she decided to use a portion of her retirement money to fund her own business. While Sarah may have spent her retirement savings, had she been aware of it, she could have avoided the terrible stress that came from feeling as though she may not be able to pay her bills the following month. She could have also immediately gotten to work laying the foundation for her business had she been aware of the capital she had to fund it, making the transition much smoother.

Financial Woman Steps

Prepare your Own and Owe Statement. Go to FinancialWoman.com/tools to get a free template.

Notice your feelings as you prepare your Own and Owe Statement. Are they empowering or disempowering?

Write out things in your life with expenses tied to them that are not on your list of money reasons, such as a large home or country club dues.

CHAPTER FOUR

YOU MEAN MY HOME COULD BE AN ASSET?

I am such a believer in bad times.

— Barbara Corcoran
Real Estate Mogul and Business Consultant

Many financial experts think that your home and mortgage should be excluded from your net worth equation. This is because a house typically creates expenses rather than revenue, and, therefore, it should not be considered an asset. Others promote that, since your home is more of a personal asset, it does not belong on your financial net worth statement. I believe that a home can be one of your largest investments; therefore, to not include it and your mortgage in your net worth equation discounts your net worth. If, however, you owe more on your mortgage than what your home is worth, excluding them would overstate your net worth. Either way, the value of your home and the amount of your mortgage are important numbers in your net worth calculation because they can greatly affect your financial picture.

RICH HABITS

Know the true marketable value of your home since it may
be your largest asset or liability.

Your Home May Be Priceless to You,
But Not Everyone Else

You may be unsure about the value to use for your home.
Since your home could be your largest asset or liability, it's
important to know its true worth. Information provided
from outside sources may not be reliable. We learned this
during the first decade of the 2000s, when appraisers were
overvaluing homes in order to allow the banks to make
larger loans against home values. Also, sometimes realtors
overstate the value with the hope of getting a listing on
your property.

Be knowledgeable about the value of your home,
whether or not you have plans to sell it in the near future.
You'll need an accurate value for your Own and Owe
Statement. Here are some suggestions for getting the real
value of your home:

- Attend open houses in your neighborhood

- Occasionally check online for recent sales of
  comparable homes in your area

- Collect sales brochures; keep them in a file so you
  can reference them

- Contact a realtor that specializes in your neighborhood to get comparable home sales; be aware that data for homes sold by owners may not be provided

Get the sales price per square foot in the information you gather. You can then take the square footage of your home and multiply it by the average sales price that you are seeing in your area. Be sure to use square footage prices for comparable homes with regards to age, condition, remodelling, location and lot size. Anything with a value as large as your home deserves a little tracking, in order to know the real value of this important asset. (Besides, don't you think it's fun to see the interior of houses in your neighborhood?)

So Many Options

By having the value of your home listed as an asset on your Own and Owe Statement, you will be more open to options regarding your home when exploring alternatives to your current financial situation. If you are an empty nester, it may be that you have a large home that is no longer necessary, or even desirable. Large homes are expensive and time-consuming to maintain. A smaller home may make more sense for you now, especially when you look at the numbers. Homes offer several different possibilities, including leasing, selling or refinancing. Given the favorable capital gains tax treatment from the sale of your primary residence, you may even consider buying homes, remodelling them over two years and then selling them.

This has been a very profitable business for some couples, especially those who consider the real estate cycle in their strategy.

If you are not yet a homeowner, play with your own housing numbers and tax rate to see if it would make sense for you to focus your money strategy on buying your first home. There are tax benefits to home ownership. Money that is used for rent instead goes to build home equity. It always makes sense to factor the real estate cycle into the decision, as well as the interest rate cycle.

Emotions are often tied to the home because of memories, but your memories and your heart are still with you wherever you live. I know of one couple who sold their large home after the kids left for college and are renting a town home until they decide where they want to live. After hearing talk about this, getting rid of a lot of my stuff and living in a smaller home sounded very liberating to me, particularly at this stage in my life. Consider what makes sense for you.

Summary

Be open-minded; look at all of your assets. Stir things up; consider changes that will allow you to reach your financial and life goals. Anything that has financial implications as large as most people's homes simply must be considered as part of your financial picture, emotions or not.

LIFE STORY

Jill and Craig were in their mid-fifties when they found themselves with an empty nest. Their house had 3 bedrooms, 2 bathrooms, a game room and pool that were rarely used since their children had left home. After discerning their own money reasons and looking at the value of their $725,000 home and the related $300,000 mortgage balance (original loan was for $500,000) with a 6.5% interest rate, they decided to make some changes. They sold their large home, generating capital of almost $400,000 after paying the mortgage in full. Then they bought a $300,000 town home, with plenty of room for visiting family in an area with a lower tax rate. They put $75,000 down and got a long term mortgage securing a 5% interest rate. As a result of the move, their monthly expenses were reduced by $2,500, as follows:

Mortgage reduction	$ 2,000
Pool maintenance	$ 200
Lawn maintenance	$ 150
Utility savings	$ 250
Housekeeper reduction	$ 100
Total reduction	$ 2,700
Increase in Homeowner's Association	-$ 200
Total monthly expense reduction	$ 2,500
Months	X12
Annual Reduced Expenses	$ 30,000
Property Tax Reduction	$ 12,000
Total Annual Savings	$ 42,000

Their property taxes were $12,000 less each year since they no longer needed to live in what was considered

continued...

the best school district, and the value of their home was half the value of their previous home. They increased the annual contribution to their investment capital by $40,000 per year. They used a portion of their annual tax savings to take their own grown children and grandchildren on an annual vacation to their favourite beach. They had more leisure time because they were maintaining a smaller home; they were accumulating more wealth, and their lives were richer in many ways.

In the case of Jill and Craig, would a financial planner or CPA have suggested all of these ideas that made their lives richer in a typical meeting? How could a financial planner know what you value most in your life after a brief meeting or two for reviewing your finances each year? Could a good financial planner or CPA clarify your ideas and point out some potential tax saving strategies once you defined your money and life goals, and you specified what you wanted to do? Absolutely, if you feel you need this support!

Financial Woman Steps

Attend open houses in your neighborhood.

Begin noticing the average sales price per square foot of homes sold in your neighborhood over the next few months.

Calculate the value of your home by using the average sales price of comparable sales per square foot for the square footage of your home.

CHAPTER FIVE

YOUR REAL NET WORTH

Awareness is everywhere. Your awareness of the unlimited potential inside of you will take you through all economic climates. Sadly, most people don't yet have this clarity.

— Sheri McConnell
CEO Smart Women's Institute, Best Selling Author

In an earlier chapter, you calculated your financial net worth. Tracking your assets and liabilities is a necessary step toward being in control of your money and regularly making sure you are on the right path to reach your financial goals. Whatever number this exercise revealed, I want to make a very important point concerning this topic.

In considering your net worth, it helps to remember that your real "worth" is so much more than the difference between your financial assets and liabilities. Your money measurement is a number, while your worth is the essence of you as a person. Your savings or capital is a measure of what you have earned and kept, thus far, in terms of money. Your worth includes so many other assets. Always be aware that your financial net worth number is where

RICH HABITS

Your real net worth is so much more than a financial number; your real net worth includes your experiences, talents, and abilities.

you are right now financially but not where you are in life. Your net worth may have declined, but you may have learned valuable information that will serve you well in the future. For example, you may have started or bought a business that you are growing, furthered the education of yourself or helped a family member. Don't ever confuse your financial net worth with your own worth or value as a person.

You are so much more than the amount of money and material things that you possess. Your true net worth includes the value of the life you have created, as well as your personal skills and experiences. If and when you question your financial situation and abilities, get out your wealth journal and make a list of all of your personal assets. Here are some categories to include:

- Experiences
- Education
- Family
- Principles
- Personality traits
- Skills

- Hobbies

- Contributions

- Careers

Be sure to include passions and knowledge in any area. As women, we often discount our most wonderful skills and talents. Some examples may include gardening, writing, car mechanics, sports, networking, leadership, fundraising, catering, child care, travel, nutrition, engineering, culture, etiquette, cooking, entertaining or shopping. The list is endless!

If you are having a hard time thinking of your personal assets, ask a few good friends. Almost everyone finds it difficult to say and write good things about themselves. Sometimes our most valuable personality traits are those that drove our parents or teachers crazy! My mother repeatedly told me that I "did not know the meaning of the word no". That trait has served me well many times during my life. Think back over your life and identify your most valuable personality traits.

Summary

Use your list of personal assets to remind you that you are much more than your financial net worth. You'll see how important this list will be to actually help you reach your financial goals when we cover this topic in the chapter on increasing your cash flow. For now, know that your value is you; you are, oh, so much more than a number!

LIFE STORY

Colleen had been working for fourteen years as a bookkeeper at a CPA firm when the firm was sold. The buyers no longer needed her services since they decided to outsource some of the work overseas. She was devastated. She struggled to find another job using the skills she had developed over the years. Colleen felt worthless; all those years as a reliable employee had led to being unemployed.

She took an inventory of her personal assets. Immediately, she saw that she had everything she needed to continue to support herself financially. In addition to being dependable and honest, she had all the skills she needed to run her own bookkeeping service. She began her own service working from home, and also in her client's offices at a higher fee. Not only was she able to choose her own hours and clients, she made 50% more income. By structuring the business as an entity, she saved a significant amount on income taxes, allowing her to put aside more money to grow. Meanwhile, she was building equity in her own company, which she could one day sell if she chose.

Financial Woman Steps

Write five of your best personality traits.

Write 3 topics in which you have vast knowledge.

Write out life experiences that created value for you, either because they brought you joy, or because you were successful.

CHAPTER SIX

CREATE A STRUCTURE THAT INVITES WEALTH

Successful money management is not a static affair.

— **Regina Leeds**
Professional Organizer, Author, Speaker

Have you ever noticed how great it feels after you organize your wardrobe? You choose a time to seriously tackle that closet and weed out all those things that no longer fit, don't match anything else, or you just don't wear. You challenge it all: the blouses, the belts, the shoes, the skirts, the jeans and the sweaters. Then, you buy bins for the things that need a storage place, so that you can easily find and assemble your wardrobe when you are rushing to get out the door. You purchase the few items that you need to complete your wardrobe, so that it is practical and refined. You know that the systems and structures you put in place will help you leave your home feeling polished and composed. Can you sense that feeling of assurance and confidence you get when you walk into your newly organized closet ahead of an important meeting or event? Why not do the same with your money?

RICH HABITS

Order encourages you to carry out the other steps of
good wealth management.

Have order and routines around your money to create
a place for your money to grow and be easily be monitored.
There is a saying that wealth does not flow to chaos. Order
allows you to more simply carry out the other steps of
good wealth management. It enables you to know quickly
how much money you have and where it is. For example,
a simple cash flow system allows you to easily see whether
you are moving toward or away from your goals each
month. Order gives you the ability to monitor and evaluate
your investments, allowing you to manage your money at
any time. Structure and systems simply make all of the
other principles easier to implement.

Systems provide a flow for documentation of financial
transactions; create them wherever possible to facilitate
easily tracking your money. Do you have months of
statements waiting to be filed? Maybe you are a meticulous
record keeper, but you have been meaning to speak with
an attorney about estate planning for years. Do you
toss unshredded documents into your garbage when,
meanwhile, you have had "buy shredder" on your to-do
list for ages? Whatever your area of weakness, schedule an
afternoon to deal with it.

Get Some Help

It takes a little time and possibly some expense for the initial implementation of creating financial systems, but, in the end, they make handling your finances easier and, therefore, growing your money will be easier; this is always a good thing. Professional organizers are available at reasonable rates to come to your office and design a system to create order; this can now be done remotely, via computer, as well. You may want to consider hiring a student for three or four hours a month to file papers and to do computer work, if this is an area where you procrastinate. This is also an excellent job for teen children because it gets the job done, while providing them with a great learning opportunity. You can then use your time for higher skilled tasks, such as learning about investing your money or implementing strategies to improve your cash flow.

If redundant tasks are not getting done, there is a reason. It doesn't matter what the reason is, but, frankly, what needs to get done is not getting done. For me, I find that tasks that are boring to me are best designated, whenever possible. I tend to enjoy the stimulating responsibilities of research and analyzing but never get around to the more mundane tasks because I just get bored. Other personalities thrive on creating order and detest research and analysis. If hiring someone to help with this is just not in your spending plan right now, swap tasks with a close friend or family member based on each of your skill sets. Whatever it takes, create a system to maintain order and sustain it based on your personality.

What does order surrounding your finances look like? We each have our own standards for the minimum that we need in order to feel like we have things under control. For one person, this may mean an immaculate and color-coded digitally labelled filing system. For another person, this may mean files that are hand labelled, legible, and allow for locating the correct information after a few tries. You know how much order you need to feel that things are under control, and, whenever necessary, you're able to easily find what you need.

Paper or Digital?

As far as paperwork goes, you may prefer a paperless system on your computer with online bank and brokerage statements, as well as tax forms. It is really about your own preferences. Whatever system you choose, be certain to make security a top priority. I resisted the transition to paperless statements for some time. I thought that paper documents would be more secure, but, after my mail was part of an FBI mail theft recovery, I decided that paperless statements may be more secure. There is certainly less shredding and filing involved. Online statements and forms make it simple to send documents to others who need them, such as a CPA. Now I use a combination of paper and electronic documents. I still like getting out a pencil and a highlighter to brainstorm some of my financial papers, occasionally, and creating my own spreadsheets from scratch. Find the system that works best and is the most comfortable to you because then you'll be more likely to use it.

Here are some suggestions for simplifying and promoting financial order:

- A filing system that is current and enables you to easily access your financial information

- A system for easily seeing what money comes in and goes out

- Safe storage of your legal documents and important financial papers

- Accessible and current legal documents

- An orderly system that allows you to track money flow

- A tax system that encourages correct and the most advantageous returns

- Documentation and required maintenance for any entities you may have for small businesses or real estate

- A regular time for emptying and dealing with email and postal mail--at least weekly

- A system that regularly backs up your computer files

- Shredding of personal financial data

- Monitoring of your credit score

Create an area for these tasks that is neat and inviting. You are more likely to spend time there if it is pleasant. Consider lighting candles, enjoying music, and creating a visually appealing space when dealing with your finances. Purchase attractive, but functional office supplies. You'll also get your tasks done more quickly if you have a quiet place, where you can shut the door and focus without outside distractions.

Systems and Structures Create Freedom

Depending on the complexity of your portfolio, following are some examples of financial management that are made easier with an orderly system.

Monitoring Cash Flow

One of the first and most basic aspects of growing your money is positive cash flow each month. This will be addressed in detail in another chapter, but I want to emphasize the important role that order plays in making this essential task an easy one. If you have an orderly foundation for the flow of money into and out of your accounts, then tracking your cash flow is simple. This is more important than ever with the many payment processing systems available now through technology, including credit cards and online banking.

Income Tax Efficiency

Another instance where order can make your financial responsibilities simpler regards your federal income taxes. For example, order includes the planning required to minimize taxes. A document with a running estimate of your projected income for the current year is helpful for good tax planning and is made easier with a simple spreadsheet. This allows for tax planning throughout the year and, additionally, contributes to paying the right amount of quarterly taxes if this is something you do.

Entity Management

As your finances become more complex, or if you start your own business, you may decide to create entities for legal and tax strategies. Entities require additional documentation, as well as income tax returns. Order becomes more important than ever with the management of entities. The more solid your initial foundation, the easier it will be to maintain financial order while moving forward on your financial journey.

Making Time for Money Matters

Financial order is not just about having a good system for financial documents and a neat office; it is also about planning and scheduling the time for tasks and meetings that are necessary for maximizing the management of your money and keeping you focused on your money goals. It's about making sure your finances remain in that "Important but Not Urgent" category. Too often these responsibilities get pushed into the "Urgent" category because they suffer neglect due to all the other tasks in the "Urgent" category. Give your money the attention it deserves; revisit your money reasons if you are struggling to get moving in this area. Remind yourself why it is important to schedule time for tending to your money.

Creating Structure Makes Life Simpler

Beyond systems for documentation and money flow, structures are the other important consideration. Create time structures for what needs to happen to accomplish financial order in relation to your money by scheduling tasks in your calendar. As a creative person, I tend to resist structure, but I have learned that it actually provides freedom and clarity. Structure, systems and routines around your money are good and seem less demanding than random attention. Also, this demonstrates that you are clearly in charge and the leader of your wealth. Examples of items to be scheduled are:

- Meetings with a CPA - two per year

- Estimation of Quarterly Tax Calculations and Payments

- Large extraordinary expenses, such as property taxes

- Annual review of estate plan, legal documents, and a meeting with your attorney, if necessary

- IRA contributions

- Annual portfolio review and rebalancing

- Biannual net worth updates

- Monthly review of account statements

- Credit card and spending plan review

- Creating your monthly household Cash Flow

- Annual, biannual or quarterly meetings with any financial professionals you use

- Client seminars provided by financial professionals you use

Your decision to invest your money on your own, or to work with an advisor, will affect the amount of time you need to spend. If you currently work with an advisor, don't let this become an excuse for not doing the many other money-related tasks of which you must take charge. You lay the foundation, and your advisor helps you with your planning and investing, depending on the type of financial professional you hire, should you choose to do so.

Summary

As much as anything, having order is about a feeling of control and confidence that accompanies it, and the solid foundation you create that invites more wealth. It lays the important baseline for you to easily see whether you are moving toward or away from your financial goals. Financial order invites confidence, assurance and more wealth.

LIFE STORY

Laura found that she never seemed to find the time to organize her finances. She was paying the bills each month, but she knew that she would put aside more money to grow if she created a system to monitor her income and her spending. She also wanted to focus on growing her retirement instead of continuing to neglect it. She turned a small closet with double doors into an inviting work space at home. She then scheduled a date with herself for the second Monday night of each month, from 8:00 to 9:00, when she would take time to review her spending from the previous month, as well as the value in her retirement account. She rewarded herself after her monthly financial review with a bubble bath and a glass of her favourite wine.

Laura also purchased a course available as an audio to learn more about the normal fluctuations in the value of her account, and how she could increase her return while managing the risk. She was able to listen to the course during her mundane daily commute, thereby increasing her financial knowledge and making the trip more stimulating at the same time. The end result of her new routine was that she felt much more financially empowered; she began to put aside more money to grow each month, as well as increase the returns on her investments. The ultimate outcome, of course, was creating the life that she wanted.

Financial Woman Steps

What areas need your attention in order to create structure and order around your money?

Write out the steps that will help you feel in control in each of these areas.

Assign a completion date for each step and put it on your calendar.

CHAPTER SEVEN

ALWAYS HAVE GOALS

Life is less about embarking on a journey to "find yourself" and more about setting goals and charting a course to "create yourself".

— **Sandra Yancey**
Founder and CEO eWomenNetwork

Create money goals, based on the "money reasons" you defined, that will lead you to what you have decided you really want in life. By having clearly defined and measurable goals, you can monitor whether you are on track to reach them, or whether you need to make changes in your money habits and investment objectives. Monitoring will help you to identify any obstacles that are getting in the way of reaching your goals and will also help you recognize your strengths that you can use to speed up the process. Remember, though, to enjoy the journey, because the journey is that thing called life. Be sure to have gratitude each day for what you do have and for what you are learning along the way to achieving your goals.

RICH HABITS

By having clearly defined and measurable goals, you can monitor whether you are on track to reach your goals, or whether you need to make changes in your money habits and investment objectives.

Align Your Money Reasons with Your Financial Goals

You should already have an idea of how much money you want based on your money reasons. Next, you'll estimate amounts that will allow you to accomplish your money reasons. From these numbers, you'll be able to create measurable goals.

The first step in this process is to look at your money reasons and estimate roughly how much money it will take to get what you want. This may involve some research on your part to see the cost of the things that you decided you really want. For example, if you want to rent a home in the French countryside for a month, do some online research to see how much that would cost. You may find that this is more attainable than you thought, once you see the prices of all the available places you can rent. Check out air fare to Paris; give some thought to the area that you would most like to see.

As you do this research, you are actively working toward making your dream become a reality. You are probably seeing some great visuals, and having some wonderful thoughts that will set your goal in your subconscious mind. Once this happens, and you give some focus to accomplishing your goals, your daily actions start being affected by your long-term goals. Your spending habits become more deliberate and conscious. Thus, your determination to put aside more money to grow drives you to create the time and focus needed to get those results, and you become committed to monitoring and evaluating your money's growth.

Apply this cost exploration to everything on your "money reason" list. If you want to make a significant financial contribution to society, for example, decide the amount and time frame necessary. If you want to send your children to college, consider whether you want out-of-state or in-state schools as an option, and the cost of tuition and living expenses you'll provide, if any. Most importantly, look at your current lifestyle. Explore whether or not you would like to leave your current job to start your own business or retire altogether. If this is a dream, decide when to make the change and how much money you'll need to live comfortably. Write these plans in your journal, adding pictures if you are a creative, visual person.

Initially, focus on the big picture amounts, and then you can delve into more concrete numbers based on the future value and expected potential returns. Spend some time writing out your goals in your journal if you enjoy handwriting. The process of writing uses both sides of the brain, so there are some benefits to handwriting important facets of our lives. You will probably also want to put them in a spreadsheet following completion, so that you can easily update your progress.

> ## Special Tip for Couples
>
> If you have a spouse, it is important that you both do this exercise since you are going to be working together toward the goals. This will tie into the "money goals" you each created earlier. If you are on the same page, your odds greatly increase for reaching your financial goals.

Time Frames on Your Journey

Be sure to include an estimated time frame for when you desire accomplishment of each goal. You will probably tweak these along the way, but by having dates associated with each of your goals, you can gauge your progress. A "guesstimate" is much better than nothing! Keep in mind: The reason for managing your money wisely is to create the life you want. When you see that you are on track, you'll receive the positive reinforcement you need to keep monitoring your earnings, your spending and your investments.

Depending on your age, you'll want to have goals for several life stages that tie into your money reasons. My suggestion is to have long term goals, such as ten years, and then shorter ones that lead you to the long term goals, such as one-, and three-year goals. You are already updating your financial net worth at least once each year as part of your ongoing plan, so you can also do an annual check to see if you are on track for your goals each year when you prepare your annual update. This process and your monthly cash flow will allow you to make changes as needed before you get too far off track. The longer out your goals are, the less clear the path will be, but without them you'll lack overall direction. You can begin with your longest term goals, and back into the shorter ones to get a gauge on where you'll need to be at the various points along your money journey.

If you find that you have fallen off track, then you'll plan the action steps to get back on track. The action steps can include looking at ways to increase your income, putting more money aside for growth with reduced spending, or combining the two. The action steps may involve learning new skills, such as more active investing, possibly in real estate or selling stock options, or they may involve researching additional revenue streams from a small business you want to start. It may include something as simple as renting out your garage apartment. You may decide that you want to reduce your lifestyle spending by moving to a smaller home, as indicated in an earlier chapter. You may tweak the focus of your business based on trend changes or change your business entirely. The variations are unlimited, and these possibilities can be tied to your career, your investment objectives or your spending habits. These are areas we'll explore more in other chapters.

Summary

The main point is that you create goals with time frames based on your money reasons. By relating your daily earning and spending patterns to what you really want it life, you'll create a path to get there. You'll then be able to create the rich life that you want.

LIFE STORY

Michelle had dreamed of going to France since she was a child. Now that she had 2 children, it seemed as though her dream would have to wait until they were grown. She discovered, however, while discerning her "money reasons", that it was important to her for her children to be able to experience a different language and culture during their childhood. The next step was to determine the cost of a trip to France, so that she could set a clear goal. She was ecstatic after finding a quaint, small cottage on an online site that rented for about the same price as the beach resort where they usually vacationed in the U.S. Next, she checked her frequent flyer miles to see if she would be able to fly her family for free using points. She learned that she had plenty of miles for this if she booked far in advance. She planned a two week trip for the following summer for about the usual cost of their family vacation. In the meantime, she began learning and teaching her children some common French phrases that they would need for their trip. After seeing the cost of the trip, she made a commitment to travel abroad with her family every two years so that they could experience other cultures together.

Financial Woman Steps

How much money do you have now?

How much money do you want in three years and why?

How much money do you want in ten years and why?

CHAPTER EIGHT

KNOW YOUR MONEY FLOW

Don't throw yourself under the bus; make spiritual health and wealth priorities.

— Kris Carr
New York Times Best Selling Author,
Motivational Speaker, Wellness Warrior

One of the most important aspects of growing your money is creating on going, positive cash flow. Once you have order around your money, it will be easy for you to do a monthly cash flow calculation for your family or household outlining money flowing in and out of your accounts. This will show you whether you are moving toward or away from your goals each month. Think of your own household as a little business and help everyone to focus on the financial well-being of that business. Think of yourself as CEO of that business; your job is to make sure that the company not only operates at a profit, but also creates and expands capital. Capital is the savings that you accumulate to invest that will compound and grow. The mission of your company is to reach your financial goals, which will allow you to obtain what you

RICH HABITS

Think of your own household as a little business while helping everyone to focus on the financial well being of that business. You are the CEO of that business. The mission of your company is to reach your financial goals; this will allow you to create the rich life that you want.

defined as your money reasons. Your money reasons will, of course, allow you to create the life that you want.

Your household cash flow is simply the money coming in and money going out each month. This should be calculated using total numbers that include everyone who contributes income and incurs expenses for your household. I use the word "household" loosely here because this may include you, your husband and five children, you and an elderly parent who lives with you, or you as a single person (who may have furry family members that have expenses but probably don't contribute any income, unless you have a dog that you breed).

Your household cash flow will guide you to your financial goals because you can easily see if you are moving toward them, with a positive number each month, or away from them, with a negative number each month. On the one hand, this task has become much more complex over the past few decades due to the multiple methods available for spending money. On the other hand, online banking helps make this an easy task, and some credit card companies allow you to download expenses into a spreadsheet. The complexity of your finances and your preferences will help you chose a system that works best for you. The main thing is that you should choose a method that you will use on a regular and ongoing basis to track the money flowing in and out of your accounts.

Create a Contingency Fund

You will most likely find that some months will have positive cash flow, while others will have negative cash flow, especially around yearend when you may have extra expenses due to the holidays and property taxes. Other events, such as major home expenses, car replacements, moves, and federal income taxes, can move you into negative territory for the month. For this reason, I suggest keeping a contingency fund for those unexpected or once-a-year unavoidable expenses, so that you can establish a regular and predictable income and expense stream. This way, you won't feel defeated in your plan to reach your goals. It's usually the unexpected that throws us off track. We all know that unexpected expenses are going to happen; we just don't know when or how much they will be. Thus, you can be prepared and feel more in control with a contingency fund, and this is what gives you financial peace.

The contingency fund is not for family ski vacations, the latest electronic device for your children during the holidays, or other optional expenses; it's for those unavoidable expenses that must be paid to maintain your standard of living. By standard of living, I don't mean a four star hotel versus a three star hotel but, rather, having a reliable car versus not having transportation or having heat versus not having heat. You get the idea; these are expenses for the things we really must have to maintain a comfortable standard of living.

Monitoring Cash Flow is Always Smart!

Even if you are fortunate to have periods when you have more income than you even want to spend each month, it's wise to monitor your monthly household cash flow. This is a smart discipline for several reasons.

Accomplish Your Money Reasons Sooner

First, you can challenge yourself to reach some of those money reason goals sooner than you thought possible. For example, if your goal is to donate a certain amount to a children's shelter by the time you are 50 years old, maybe you can do it when you are 47, simply by spending smarter. You may find yourself thinking that, instead of spending that $100 on yet another "doodad" you don't need, you'd rather the money go toward books at the children's shelter.

Feel Good About Spending Your Money

Second, tracking your money helps you to feel good about what you do spend and keeps you from spending money on things that really don't matter. When you monitor your spending, you naturally spend more consciously. Just try it; it really makes a difference when you know you are going to have to reduce your cash flow number for yet another pair of black shoes, when you have challenged yourself to reach a certain amount of positive cash flow for the next month.

Spending Expands To Fill the Gap

Money is like time; it fills a vacuum. Our spending will grow to suit our income, just as our time expands to fill whatever block we have allotted for completing a task. I am not asking you to be stingy and frugal in monitoring your spending; spending creates jobs and opportunities for others. I am suggesting that you spend wisely and consciously.

High Income Periods Could End

The last reason for calculating your monthly cash flow is that the high income periods of our lives often don't last forever. There are exceptions to this, of course, such as royalties and income from passive business ownership or real estate, but, even then, the unexpected can happen. It is hard to imagine during your prime earning years that your skills could become obsolete (which is happening more and more with new technology) or that the company that pays you so well could terminate your employment or go bankrupt. Unfortunately, both of these scenarios happen on a regular basis.

If and when your income does meet an unexpected bump in the road, you'll be much better prepared to navigate through challenging times if you are accustomed to tracking your spending. By monitoring your monthly cash flow, you will maximize your wealth potential during those high income years. By spending sensibly during those periods, it will be easy to transition to lower income periods, if and when necessary. Even if you know you will never spend all of your money, spending consciously allows you to leave more money as your legacy. The bottom line is that it always makes sense to monitor your spending and have a plan that leads to your financial goals and beyond.

Invite Your Money to Grow

Always challenge yourself for the maximum amount that you can put away for your wealth foundation capital each month. Put this amount into your cash flow as an expense, labelled with a name that inspires you, such as "My Wealth." The idea is to reach a comfortable lifestyle and have your monthly cash flow near zero each month, including the maximum amount you can put aside to grow. This will allow you to accumulate wealth.

Summary

One of the most important actions in good wealth management is monitoring how much money comes in and how much goes out every month, then reviewing the sources of those amounts. Set up a regular time to calculate these numbers, print them, and look at them over a cup of coffee, pen in hand, to see how you can make them better.

This is your role as CEO of your own money business. Once you begin using a simple spreadsheet to track these items, it only takes a little time to update it each month. Know that this is a big step in leading you to your financial goals because it will show you very clearly whether you move toward or away from your financial goals each month.

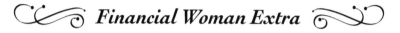

Financial Woman Extra

Go to **FinancialWoman.com/tools**
for a free visual Money Flow chart to clarify the
importance of this step.

LIFE STORY

Ingrid was able to pay all of her bills each month fairly easily. In fact, her salary as an attorney allowed for her to buy much more than the minimum she needed be happy. She felt confident in her earning abilities; however, at age thirty-seven she had very little money in her investment account. She also had never purchased a home, so she always had an unsettled feeling about her financial future. She decided she was ready to change that. After spending only an hour calculating her cash flow from the previous month, she saw that money was carelessly going out. She also realized that she was paying a lot of money in income taxes. When an opportunity arose the next month for her to purchase a home near her sister that she had admired for years, she decided to buy it. While she would live a little further from her work, the house payments were considerably less than her downtown rent had been, and she would have the tax benefits of home ownership. Without having tracked her cash flow the month prior, she would have probably not even considered investing in the house. She loved the yard, and the fact that she could now get a dog. More importantly, she could spend more time with her sister's family. The steps she took for financial empowerment definitely led to a richer life.

Financial Woman Steps

List all of your expenses from last month.

Make a list of all of your income from last month.

Did you move toward or away from your wealth goals last month?

CHAPTER NINE

BRAINSTORM WAYS TO INCREASE YOUR INCOME

What is the simplest direct path to increase my income?

— **Ali Brown**
CEO Ali International LLC,
ABC's Secret Millionaire, Inc. 500 ranking

If your expenses outweigh your income, then one of two things will get you back on track in order to reach your goals: You can either increase your income or lower your expenses, or do both. This is a simple truth that is often avoided. In this chapter, we'll address the first side of the equation, which is increasing the amount that you earn. Once you develop a mindset around this, there is a good chance that ideas and options to increase your cash flow with additional income will begin to surface. Increasing your income can be accomplished through creating additional revenue sources from your work, from your saved capital, or from both.

Consider Starting Your Own Business

The great news is that we are in an incredible time to create additional sources of revenue due to technology. When the

RICH HABITS

We are in a remarkable time to create additional sources of income through the use of technology. Use your talents and skills to earn income, while also giving to society.

Forbes® 400 consists of numerous young people who formed businesses in college, or shortly thereafter, with very little or no capital, you know you are living in a time of incredible opportunity. A business can be formed literally with well under $100 by creating a word press blog on a computer at the public library. Research is available for free on the internet. Passion and determination are much of what is called for to become a successful business person today. Previously, it cost thousands of dollars to form only the smallest business, and this often required a huge financial commitment for a lease and equipment. Opportunity abounds to increase your income based on your skill sets and knowledge. The most challenging component may be time, especially if you have a full-time job, children, or elderly parents that need extra attention and care, but numerous successful businesses have been created under these circumstances.

This concept relates to the "earn" part of the "earn, grow, give" equation as much as it relates to the "give" part. The beautiful thing about this principle is that, when you create a business based on your talents with the intention of increasing your income, you are also giving of yourself; you are contributing to society with your special gifts, skills and abilities. You will then give on another level by paying the people you hire to help in your business, and then, again, with the resources for goods and services that you spend as you grow your business. Charitable giving is only one part of the giving element.

There are countless stories of women who began businesses based on their skill-set and an unmet need that they saw while they were at home raising children or working. Examples include fashionable fabric swaddles for carrying a baby, a gadget that makes it impossible for a toddler to unroll the toilet paper off of the holder, and organic food products. Amilya Antonetti invented a line of natural cleaning products after noticing that her son became very ill right after her home was cleaned. Kendra Scott passionately created a jewellery empire after taking a few samples to local stores made from the last of her savings, while carrying her swaddled baby. Businesses that went on to become multi- million dollar enterprises were built on a talent, an idea, and a commitment. Perhaps that talent was the valuable knowledge and insight of which idea to develop and market. Maybe the talent was making jewellery, inventing, creative branding or cooking.

What are your talents? Look back at the personal assets that you discerned in an earlier chapter of this book. How many times have you had an idea that you didn't pursue and then you saw the product in a store? Think big and creative. If being an entrepreneur appeals to you, get out a journal and begin writing your ideas and a one-page business plan.

Options for Employees

If you work for someone else, good strategies to increase your income include:

- Asking for a raise

- Moving to a different company with higher pay

- Learning a new skill that will increase your pay scale

- Returning to school to increase your pay scale

- Setting up shop as a consultant doing what you are already doing at a higher fee

The Consultant vs. Employee Model

There is a good chance the company you work for will continue to hire you if you should decide to use a consulting structure. There are several benefits to becoming a consultant that offset the risk of owning your own business. This business model will give you the opportunity to begin working with other clients outside of your current employer.

Lower employer costs can equate to higher earnings for you

If you are married and covered under a spouse's insurance policy, this may be even more advantageous to your employer since you can lower their cost of having you as a full-time employee. The tax benefits of being set up as an independent contractor, along with higher consulting fees, will most likely make this a more profitable way for you to work.

Gain flexibility with your hours and location

Technology gives you the opportunity to do some, if not all, of the work from a home office at a relatively low start-up cost. Former commuting time can be spent as earning time. Consider starting your business on the side and build up a clientele before leaving your job, so that you can test the market and establish a client base. You would want to have at least six to nine months of living expenses saved beforehand, depending on the number of dependents you have. Not to suggest that a man is a plan, but, if you are married and your spouse has a secure job, this transition is easier. Regardless, make sure you have some capital on which you can live during the lean times.

Create equity in your own company

Another benefit if you are a consultant is that you will be growing your own company instead of someone else's company. Your skills are initially much of the value of your company, but after a few years, your client list will be valuable. Additionally, if you hire staff who assumes some or all the work load, your business equity increases. This will also allow you to leverage your skills and ability so you can grow your company.

Lower your income taxes with entity structure

One more important point about creating a consulting practice or other small business with the intention of generating income is that tax advantages exist when you use an entity structure for your business. Should you decide to start your own business, it is important to set it up correctly from a taxation and legal standpoint. This can be done either through an attorney and a CPA, or with an online legal documentation provider if you have knowledge in this area.

Once you clearly set your intention to increase your income, you will begin to develop a new mindset. Be open to opportunities that appear in whatever form they may appear. You may decide it makes sense to invest more in income-producing assets right now. Maybe an advertisement for a workshop on creating your own business will cross your path, or maybe you will decide to use your skills to get involved with real estate properties. You may finally decide to find a job that pays you what you are worth instead of compromising.

Summary

There are so many possibilities available to increase your income. Refer back to the list of personal assets that you created in an earlier chapter. Brainstorm ways that you can share your talents and skills to increase your income. Be open to all possibilities. Again, be creative and bold; think big and outside of the box. Step into being who you need to be to get and give what you want in your life. And while you're at it, why not create a rich life full of the things that you value and enjoy?

LIFE STORY

Melissa was working as an interior designer at a home décor shop. The customers loved her and, as a result, frequently requested her help while selecting products. Customers began asking her if she did work on the side, and she always said that she did not. Melissa analyzed her monthly cash flow and saw that she would not reach her financial goals without a significant increase in income.

She decided to start her own interior design business. She created a logo and ordered business cards online. She had a friend create a website. The cost was well under $200. Two weeks later, she approached her employer and explained that she was beginning her own interior design business. She explained that she still wanted the store to provide many products that she would suggest for her clients. She asked if she could continue to provide her services on a consulting basis. The owner agreed, recognizing the value she brought to the store.

It was no longer necessary for Melissa to remain in the store as a sales person, thereby allowing her to work fewer hours but at a much higher rate. She was also able to eventually supply additional products that she got for her customers directly from suppliers, while maintaining a good relationship with the store where she had worked. The rewards, both near and long-term, were great for a low amount of risk.

Financial Woman Steps

What are three possible opportunities to increase your income?

Which of the three opportunities is the simplest to implement?

Write out the steps for implementing the simplest income- generating idea.

CHAPTER TEN

ALLOWING YOUR MONEY
TO GENERATE INCOME

Investment success is not about following the right predictions.
It's about following the right principles.

— **Alex Green**
Chief Investment Strategist Investment U,
Wall Street veteran and Best Selling Author

The second way to increase your income is by investing your capital in assets that generate income. Keep in mind that you wouldn't want to permanently live off of the investment returns of the money you have set aside to compound unless you have deliberately entered the retirement phase of your life. In other words, if you decide to pay bills with your investment income, you have made a conscious decision to live off of your investments.

Living off of investment income usually occurs for two different reasons. First, you may be financially in a place where you can do this with enough funds to generate income to cover your living costs for the rest of your life. If you can, then you are truly wealthy. The second reason that investors live off of investment income is often due to

RICH HABITS

If you are paying your bills with investment capital or investment income, then you have made a decision to live off of your investments.

a temporary life circumstance. This is frequently due to job loss or a lifestyle change that mandates a temporary period of reduced or no income. During periods of low interest rates, investors must sometimes also withdraw capital to pay bills if they based their financial plan on higher interest rates. During such times, it makes sense to actively seek higher income producing strategies, within acceptable risk levels, to limit the amount of capital withdrawal.

The most common traditional income generating methods are:

- Common stock dividends

- Preferred stocks dividends

- Real estate investment trust (REIT) dividends

- Bond interest

More alternative income producing methods include:

- Oil and gas holdings

- Real estate rental ownership

- Option selling

Covered Call Writing

Covered call writing is a common option strategy in which a call option is sold against stocks that are held in the account. Frequently, the call option will expire without being exercised, and the owner of the stock simply keeps the option premium. This technique is used by funds, as well as individual investors, to generate income from stock portfolios.

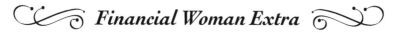

Financial Woman Extra

To receive a free handout about this strategy,
go to: **FinancialWoman.com/tools.**

A Word of Caution

Many investors think that bonds are safe investments. One very important factor to remember is that, in general, the higher the yield, the more the value of the asset will decline when interest rates increase. This is referred to as an "inverse relationship" in investing lingo. Higher yields generally apply to longer term commitment for that yield, such as a 30 year bond versus a 3 year bond. The relationship is very logical; the asset value decreases because investors can get a higher yield on newer assets. Assets paying the older, lower market rates for a long time, therefore, will decline in value. This interest rate risk applies especially to long-term bonds, as well as other high-yield type of investments, such as REITs and oil and gas trusts, to a lesser extent.

Pay Attention to the Economy

There are good and bad times to invest in most income producing categories in conjunction with the economic cycle. Different income producing strategies work best during different phases of the economic cycle. Market interest rates affect the income or yield you can expect to receive from different asset classes. Inflation must also be considered since it reduces the purchasing power of the income you receive. The challenge with investment income is choosing a method that allows a generous amount of income, while also allowing an acceptable amount of principle risk. Sometimes it makes more sense to aim for capital appreciation or growth as an investment objective instead of income, even if this means that you will withdraw capital. The question to consider is: where will you get the best return for your money within an acceptable risk level?

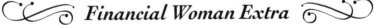 *Financial Woman Extra*

Visit **FinancialWoman.com/tools**
for a free hand-out on the different investment
objectives, such as capital appreciation and growth.

Summary

As you can see, the desired outcome from your money ties back to the investment objectives for the assets on your Own and Owe Statement, financial goals, and the time frame for reaching those goals. The amount of capital and the available level of income from that capital vary depending where you are in your money journey and, also, the economic cycle. It is important to realize that you have much control over the former and no control over the latter. Be diligent in controlling what you can: your money journey. Do this by maximizing the earnings and growing potential of your money, while realizing that factors beyond your control can affect the results of each. Knowledge of how those factors affect your money, and being proactive with that knowledge reduces the risk from those uncontrollable economic factors.

This discussion leads to the following habits that are covered throughout this book: Monitor and maximize your earnings potential by seeking ways to best capitalize on your skill sets. Maximize your monthly cash flow by monitoring spending and adjusting as needed. Put aside as much capital to grow as you are able, while maintaining an acceptable living standard. Know how much money you have to invest, where it is, and understand the basics of how it is invested. Develop an awareness of the economy and how it affects your money. Be proactive, knowledgeable and accountable. Create a rich life.

LIFE STORY

Judy retired from her corporate job at age 58 with investment capital of $1,500,000. She had eased into a private consulting practice that generated net income of $5,000 per month as her corporate job ended. Now that she had more time to devote to her consulting practice, she would be able to take on a few more clients from the backlog of people who had expressed a desire to work with her. In the meantime, she decided to allocate $300,000 of her investment capital to a strategy that produced income at a rate of 12%. This provided $3,000 a month to use toward her living expenses, which totalled around $8,000 each month. She planned to grow her business over the next year to increase her income to over $8,000 a month. At that time, she would apply the approximate $300,000 investment capital back toward capital appreciation as an investment objective, since she would no longer need the extra income to live comfortably. This would allow her to grow her money and accumulate more for later in life when she would choose to stop working altogether.

Financial Woman Steps

Check to see if you have any investments with values that are closely tied to the interest rate cycle.

Look at your long term goals to estimate when you will want to live off of your investment capital.

Review your investments to determine whether the main objective is to generate income or to appreciate in value.

CHAPTER ELEVEN

ADJUST YOUR SPENDING PLAN

If you are faithful with your time, you will be a ruler with much more time. If you can be faithful with the money you are given, you can be ruler over much more money. If you can be faithful with the influence you have, you will be given much more influence.

— **Dani Johnson**
Best Selling Author, Multiple Business Owner,
ABC's Secret Millionaire, homeless at age 21

Now, let's explore the other side of the cash flow equation: Your spending patterns. When all of the bills can easily be paid, you can quickly lose track of your spending, but by becoming a conscious spender it's likely that you will be able to knock off a few expenses. In regards to reducing your spending, the term "spending plan" is a lot more appealing than "budget." Think of it like this: you have a certain amount of money coming in each month, and your spending plan outlines how you choose to spend that money. This feels much more empowering than the thought of having to live on a budget because you don't have enough money every month.

RICH HABITS

Everyone knows that finding good value is just plain fun. Take this natural instinct and turn it into a habit that keeps your monthly cash flow positive; enjoy the pleasure in the smart use of your resources.

Think Conscious and Wise, Not Cheap and Frugal

Focusing on reducing expenses can be as fun as generating more income, particularly since it usually just involves a mindset shift, and not necessarily more work. I definitely promote conscious and wise spending, and I prefer this attitude over cheap and frugal. During those leaner times in my life, I have found the following mindsets helpful.

Look How Far You've Come

Think about how much money you made earlier in your life when you earned less, and compare that to your current household monthly income. I still remember that I modelled and sold shoes for less than three dollars an hour in my early teens. In my first job after college, I made $13,060 a year. Of course, I didn't stay a year because, after three months, I found a much better position making the larger salary of $16,030 with better benefits, including a stock plan. Even though inflation has to be factored into that number to make it relative to today's dollars, I am now far ahead of that number, thankfully. However, I know that I managed to live just fine on the previous salaries; this thought empowers me.

Recognize That It's Just Plain Fun

Have an attitude that makes reduced spending a pleasure. As someone who loves the challenge of finding good value in anything, whether it is an undervalued piece of real estate, a company stock, or a piece of my favourite John Hardy® jewellery, I truly believe that living within your spending plan is a mindset that can be enjoyed. Below is an example of what I mean.

I like to take a look at the resale shop when I drop off my better clothes because, years ago, I discovered one of my favourite all time purchases hanging in the window at the consignment store: a tan Banana Republic four-ply, brand-new cashmere sweater for twenty dollars. This was about nine years ago, and it is still one of my favourite pieces, not only because of its classic design and good quality, but because I recall the purchase with pleasure every time I pull it out to wear. Why? Because finding good value is just plain fun, and this means that being a smart and conscientious spender is enjoyable. Through researching the spending patterns of women, I have learned that women, especially, like good value, and they also love to share their finds with others to help them get good value. Take this natural instinct and turn it into a talent that keeps your monthly cash flow positive and guides you to your financial goals by finding the pleasure in smart spending.

Develop a Value Based Mindset

Enjoy the treasure hunt and apply it to bigger purchases in your life. For example, you can save thousands by purchasing a low mileage, used, good-quality car instead of a new one that depreciates five percent when you drive it off the lot. You can buy a foreclosed property needing some TLC as an investment or as a home. Develop and use a mindset of always buying value, especially on higher priced assets, to get to your financial goals sooner.

Practice Gratitude

Have gratitude for what you do have. Think of all the people in the world who would gladly swap places with you. Instead of feeling frustrated that you can't be a member of the top country club right now, appreciate that you can play golf at a wonderful public course or swim at a neighborhood pool or at a beautiful lake. Always focus on what you do have, not on what you are lacking. There is always more to accumulate, and focusing on what you don't have will always leave you feeling needy. Live in a place of gratitude to expand your wealth mindset.

Get Out of Your Box

Realize that your level of wealth is all completely relative. In the above example, the person who cannot spend on the country club membership doesn't have an awareness of the person who would love to be able to just buy golf clubs. The person flying first class, who is unhappy because she cannot fly charter, doesn't see the person who would give anything to be able to fly instead of drive for the family vacation, or even take a family vacation. The person who flies charter really wishes she could have her own plane. The person who settles for organic food at home instead of dining out is unaware of the person who would give anything to be able to buy organic food for her family but can't because it costs more than conventional food. There are countless examples of these separate little boxes of lifestyle spending habits. Boxes keep you trapped and can create negative emotion around your money. Get out of your own little box and step back a box or two to have true gratitude for what you do have because, no matter what box you are in, there will always be a bigger, better and more enticing one.

Focus on the Big Picture

With regards to your spending, don't be penny wise and pound foolish. Some people say to watch the pennies, and the dollars will take care of themselves. I say, "Watch the dollars, and the pennies will take care of themselves." By focusing on the big picture first, such as knowing your monthly money flow and knowing why you want money, your intentions will trickle down to your everyday spending, almost on an unconscious level.

Let me give you an example of how this happens: If you have decided that you are going to reduce your spending so that you can accumulate more wealth based on your big money reasons and your current money flow, you don't have to agonize when you see the black boots that you don't need on sale (and that may even require the use of credit to purchase) because you have made a higher-level decision. In fact, you probably won't even be in the store because you are living your life on purpose, and you are spending your time on something of quality that leads to your overall life plan. You may even be spending former shopping time relaxing and reading your favourite financial publication on your porch, updating your monthly family cash flow, or researching a new business idea at the bookstore. This isn't about owning black boots (which I happen to love!); it's about using your time, energy, and money on things that you don't need or truly even care about owning, relative to other things in life.

A Few Smart Spending Tips

By simply reviewing your monthly spending, you'll likely find several areas where you can save money with very little effort, if any. Here are just a few of my favourite ideas you may want to consider, some of which will make sense for almost everyone to reduce their spending:

- Buy good quality, low mileage used cars
- Simply pay attention to your water and energy usage
- Scrutinize your credit card bills for unauthorized charges
- Hire students to do work, such as yard and office work
- Plan everything, especially meals and travel
- Build your wardrobe around jeans, black pants and one neutral suit
- Buy classic style late season

- Proactively reduce your income taxes

- Stretch car ownership for another year or two

- Use online sites for lodging during travel

- Stay at inns and wineries while traveling abroad

- Buy what you need

- End shopping as a hobby

Always keep the mindset that smart spending is fun!

Summary

If you did not like the spending pattern you saw from your monthly household cash flow calculation, first revisit your childhood money beliefs to see if you are acting in ways that validate those old and invalid beliefs. If you are, then choose your own money beliefs and establish habits that support those beliefs. Second, put a little note in your wallet that you will see every time you make a purchase. When you see the note, ask yourself if that purchase is a conscious one or not; you can always change your mind. Third, focus on having gratitude for what you do have to live in a state of abundance, instead of lack, as you spend less. By having gratitude, your spending plan will become a blessing rather than a curse, and your life will become a pleasant journey rather than a struggle.

LIFE STORY

Nina had always purchased new cars, just as her mother had done. She had never questioned this practice until she began tracking her spending. She realized that over the years, she had spent a lot of money on new cars. She would replace them once they reached 55,000 miles, which was usually after driving them for around three years. The amount of sales tax on the cars was also a big chunk of money. She usually got less than half of what she had paid for the car when she "traded" it for a new one at the dealer. Nina's friend had sold her car online, and had gotten considerably more than the amount that had been offered by the dealership. Nina heard about a car dealer that specialized in good quality used cars. The cars came with a guarantee, and the dealer had an excellent reputation in her community. She decided to purchase a car from the dealer for $26,000 which had only 18,000 miles on the odometer. It was a better quality brand of car than she had been able to previously own; therefore, it would have a higher resale value when she wanted to replace it. The body was the same as the new model at another dealer, which sold for $38,000. She felt certain that she would be able to drive the used car for at least 100,000 miles given the brand.

She obtained a quote from the dealer to trade her old car for $15,000. She then listed her car on the same online site that her friend had used for a price for $18,000. She felt this was a fair price based on the

continued...

recent sales she saw online for similar cars. She was thrilled when she sold it a week later for $ 17,500. Nina calculated that she had reduced the cost of buying a new car by around $ 15,000, including tax. Since she projected that she could drive the car for about two years longer than her previous cars, the amount she would save in the long term would be substantial. She realized that if she had used this method for the past six car purchases, she would have at least another $ 100,000 in savings. She could have also driven a better quality car.

Nina decided that this had been a good but expensive insight gained from paying attention to how she spent her money. Looking ahead, she planned to always use this method. Not only did it allow her to grow more money, it was fun! She couldn't wait to find other areas of her life where she could decrease her spending, improve the quality of her belongings, and at the same time, increase her wealth!

Financial Woman Steps

Write in your wealth journal about a time when you made or had less money than you have now.

Explore your spending to find three areas where you are not spending consciously.

Write out specific steps you will take to move toward conscious spending in the three areas you discovered.

CHAPTER TWELVE

ALWAYS BE PREPARED TO TAKE OVER YOUR FINANCES

I will not let my finances happen to me anymore. I will determine my income. I will take all of that power back.

— **Carrie Wilkerson**
Barefoot Executive Founder and CEO

This one can seem a little scary, but the truth is that no one plans for the unexpected. Maybe you are fully responsible for your finances right now, but I frequently speak with women who are avoiding their money. Avoidance can take place because a financial advisor is used, a spouse or other family member manages your money, or money is just blindly placed into cash or funds.

There are several reasons for being prepared to take over the management of your money at any time, beyond the unexpected happening in your life. For instance, just knowing that you can step into any important role, especially one that affects the quality of your life as much as money does, is empowering. Things just feel bigger and scarier when we don't know anything about them. Think of all the experiences in your life that you dreaded because

RICH HABITS

Get comfortable with managing your finances during a normal time of your life. Statistics show that, if you are a women, there is a 90% likelihood that you will be solely in charge of your finances at some point during your life.

they seemed big and intimidating, and then, after you learned how to do them, you wonder why you had been so intimidated by them.

The second reason that you need to be ready to step into your wealth management is reinforced by numbers: Studies reveal that ninety percent of women will solely be responsible for their money at some time in their life. My father left this world in 1993 somewhat suddenly following a brief battle with a brain tumour. While my brother and I did not know everything we needed to know at the time, I am so grateful we knew enough to help my mother with her finances. She had been financially empowered throughout their long marriage and was able to easily pass the responsibility to us while she allowed herself time to grieve.

Unfortunately, sometimes a woman suddenly learns that she has much less money than she thought that she had when a spouse is lost from either divorce or death. There are so many women who are left alone without ever having been involved with their money management. Often they don't have grown children who are able or knowledgeable to step in and provide support in this area. During this time, the last thing a woman wants to do is worry about where her money is and how she will pay her bills.

Third, by being capable financially, we are sending a message to the next generation of women that it is important to be knowledgeable and involved with personal wealth management. Generation by generation this typically unspoken stigma is being reduced, but it is still out there, alive and well. An empowered woman of this century knows where her money is and demonstrates competence around it. This is how we want our daughters, nieces and our friend's daughters to feel, not fear or dependence. Do we want them banking on the old "a man is a plan" theory that is both false and disempowering?

Dated Attitudes

There have been several times since I began my financial education business for women that men have made snide remarks involving their wives and money, while other (more confident and secure perhaps?) husbands have encouraged their wives to work with me. When they have been discouraging, it seemed as though they had spoken before they even realized it, and they sometimes have seemed embarrassed afterward. There are still unrecognized beliefs remaining from the days (not too long ago) when women left the room when money was discussed.

Let me share a couple of examples of what I mean: I was once at a luncheon in Austin where Ben Bernanke was the speaker. I was seated with a couple in their sixties, their grown son, a female financial advisor, who was hosting our table, along with two other female clients. The married woman inquired about my work, and I explained that I help women learn about money and investing. She seemed interested in this concept, but her husband found it so funny that he shared it with his son, who was sitting next to him. The two of them got a great laugh out of the absurd thought of a woman learning about managing her money. Who looked like the fool? The sad thing is that the woman felt embarrassed and intimidated. She lacked the confidence to stand up to him on this topic, but she will very likely wish one day that she knew more about managing her finances. The statistics report that it is likely that she will be in charge of the family money at some point in her life.

Another time I was at a speaker's conference when a man in his early sixties asked me what type of work I was doing. When I told him that I taught women about money and investing, amidst his chuckling he responded that I should teach his wife. Knowing exactly where the conversation was headed, I asked him why his wife needed help with money. He explained that they had been shopping for new furniture the day before. At this point, he became somewhat embarrassed. He went on to explain that she had negotiated zero percent interest for twenty months on their purchase and had also recently bought a car on her credit card with no interest for a similar period of time. He then acknowledged that she was actually pretty savvy with money, but only after having first jumped right into the "women are money-ignorant" routine that is still common today.

Let's look at a few of these statistics: [1]

- Ninety percent of women will be solely responsible for their finances at some point in their lives.

- Fifty percent of all U.S. investment capital comes from women.

- Women have shorter work lives than men. On average, women take the equivalent of eleven years out of the workforce to care for family members.

- Seventy-three percent of women define wealth as security or freedom.

- A survey of American households done by Iowa State University found that when couples didn't make investment decisions together, the men overwhelmingly took control.

Others from Liz Perle [2] include:

- 55% of married women bring in half of the household income and 25% now out earn their spouses.

- Women routinely don't save enough to survive on when they become widows –which 50% of us will be by the age of 60.

- One survey from the National Center for Women and Retirement showed that of those women who say they feel in control of their lives, 56% of them

---

1 Citigroup. Women & Co.
2 Perle, Liz. Money, a Memoir. Women, Emotions and Cash. New York. Henry Holt, 2006

saved and invested monthly. Of the 42% who said they felt out of control, only 17% made saving and investing for retirement a priority.

- There's a direct correlation between how well a woman takes care of herself financially and how well she feels about herself.

- In the last decade alone, more than $8 trillion transferred to a younger generation – more than 55% of which went to women.

- When asked, 70% of men in one UC Irvine study felt they were entitled to earn more than anyone else while a similar percentage of women said they should earn what others earned. But most revealing, 85% of men said they knew what they were worth. A similar number of women responded that they weren't sure.

- 38% of women 30-55 years old are worried they will live at or near the poverty level because they cannot adequately save for retirement. The figure increases to 53% for women of color. For men, 33% face the same dilemma.

Summary

As you can see, the overwhelming odds show that you will one day be solely responsible for your finances. Why not get more comfortable with them during a "normal" time in your life if you are not already involved? If this reason alone is not enough to get you to embrace your financial journey, then focus on creating the life that you want to have. You are almost certainly involved with the spending of your financial resources, which is a huge part of the equation when considering your cash flow. Allocate some time toward managing and growing your money so you can feel confident and capable on this essential topic that greatly determines your quality of life.

LIFE STORY

Charlene's husband, Jack, had always managed their money. He paid the bills, handled the banking, met with the CPA, and made the investment decisions. He showed her their investment account statements, but she always felt she was too busy to become involved, with her job, managing their home and children. One day, Jack found out that he had a terminal illness. The last thing Charlene wanted to do was to start learning about their finances. Three days after his funeral, Charlene had to meet with their CPA, so that she could pay the bills that had been arriving, already marked late, and start being in charge of her finances. They scheduled three more meetings over the next month with the CPA and his bookkeeper to increase Charlene's involvement and go through her documents. It was costly and, more importantly, terribly disruptive during the time that she wanted to spend grieving.

Financial Woman Steps

Notice what feelings and thoughts arise when you think of solely being in charge of your money.

Do these feelings need to change?

If the answer is yes, what specific steps do you need to take to feel more confident about being responsible for your money?

PART TWO

STEPS YOU MUST TAKE FOR GROWING YOUR MONEY

CHAPTER THIRTEEN

OWN THAT IT
IS YOUR MONEY

Do it whether you want to or not; Don't think about it. If it has to be done, just do it.

— **Rhonda Britten**
Emmy Award winner,
Best Selling Author, International Speaker

In an earlier chapter you discovered the importance of defining your own money reasons. This is a very personal issue. Maybe you realized that money is important because you want to contribute to society through your financial gifts; you want a second home near your favourite ski run; or you want to spend your days doing as you please (which may exclude a daily commute in traffic). You now clearly know your reasons for wanting money, and wanting money ultimately means managing your money well. Your personal money reasons lead you to the "why" and provide the motivation to create good money habits.

Once you embrace that the outcomes you desire from your money are your choices alone, not those of a family

RICH HABITS

Learn just 1% about the huge topic of money and investing to be able to confidently manage or oversee your money management. You already do this in many areas of your life as a woman.

member or a financial professional you may use, it becomes clear that no one cares about your money as much as you do. This obvious fact can be easily evaded, particularly if you don't personally handle your finances or invest your money. This can be true even if you are involved with the decision of where to invest. When someone else is managing your finances for you, whether a family member, a fund manager or a financial advisor, it seems that they are responsible for your money, and not you. After all, they are spending their time, or you may be paying them a fee for doing so, and this buys you the right to back away, right? Yes and no. While you may be alleviated from the weekly or monthly management of your financial accounts, you are not relieved from being involved with the oversight of the management. There is a fine but important balance between allowing someone else to manage your finances and, at the same time, staying in charge of your money. You are the person whose life would be affected by the loss of your money. In cases of financial professionals, your advisor or fund manager may lose a customer, but you could lose your lifestyle and/or your home. By acknowledging this, you can see that you are clearly the one responsible for your own money, and that no one else cares about your money more than you do. In regards to a spouse managing your finances, I highly encourage couples to share both financial goals and responsibilities, as you have seen throughout this book.

While working with financial professionals, there can be a feeling of intimidation concerning the fact that you are just a regular person with very little or no knowledge of finances or investing, attempting to monitor the person you chose to manage your money. You know that this financial professional knows a lot more about money than you do and probably even has "credentials." Credentials, however, don't necessarily mean that you are getting the best results for the level of risk you are taking, or that you are on the way to reaching your financial goals.

You Don't Have to Learn It All!

Beyond making sure that you put aside money to grow, staying in charge of your money requires educating yourself enough to oversee the management of the money that you have accumulated for growth. It also requires the discipline to stay somewhat knowledgeable about the changing economy that drives the value of your investments. Know enough to feel empowered rather than intimidated when taking charge of your money. By learning one percent of the enormous topic of "wealth management", you can do this. This necessary education may begin by reading books or taking a course. You can then choose some simple ways to stay current on an ongoing basis about what is happening in the economy that will affect the value of your investment accounts.

When you learn just one percent of almost any topic, then you can wisely oversee management of something by someone else, but that one percent is absolutely crucial to know in order to do an adequate job of oversight. By thinking about how true this is in other areas of your life, whether it is providing an education for your child, remodelling your home, or owning a passive company, you'll realize that this principle should also apply to your money management. Unfortunately, many people don't apply it, especially women. For some reason, women often feel intimidated when stepping into the leadership role of wealth management, yet they valiantly lead in many other areas of their lives. I think this is especially true when women have been outside of a work environment for many years. Let's look at some common examples where women automatically learned the one percent necessary to lead projects in their lives.

For example, you don't learn all of the details applicable to educating your child; you don't learn the eighth grade curriculum. You may find out the best math curriculum and ask whether it is used at the school you are considering. You don't learn how to install new flooring in your home if you are remodelling. You learn one or two percent of the subject, like the advantages of wood versus tile flooring. Then, you hire someone or make decisions based on what you learned, but, without the one percent, you wouldn't know who to hire, or whether he would do a good job. A "good job" is not all you are seeking though, is it? You want an excellent job in each of these areas. You want your child's education to be top-notch and your floors to be perfect, just like you want excellent results from your investments.

Another example can be applied to running a company. Even if you outsource almost all of the work in the company, you still need to know the fundamentals of the business to be a truly capable manager, to run the company at peak performance and to maximize profits. The larger the company, the less the CEO knows about the details of each division, but she definitely knows the big picture.

Give the same amount of energy and leadership to your money management as you give to other areas of your life. Why would you not? Learn the one percent about investing and become comfortable with those few fundamentals. Knowledge of those fundamentals is what will get you where you want to be and give you confidence during the journey.

Always be aware that money is what provides that new flooring, the education (either through taxes or private tuition), and the capital to build or buy the company in the above examples. It provides much more than that, too: Money is what provides the basic primary needs in life, like food and shelter. Why, then, is tending to our money so often not even on our "to do" list? Without food and shelter, let's face it, life is not too grand. In fact, you cannot even live without food for long! I encourage you to give money its due attention through devoting your time and energy to learning one percent about managing and investing it.

Clarify Your Priorities

Now take this one minute exercise:

Write down five areas of your life that are most important to you.

Was money on your list? If not, maybe it should be. Many of us, especially in the United States, take for granted food and shelter; however, my guess is that it would be near the top of your list if you had considered it. If you wrote family as a priority, it is likely that food and shelter would be part of that equation, whether or not you wrote it. Maybe success in your career was on that list. While the joy of a career well done is unquestionably a worthy goal, the associated compensation is likely a valuable reward. Isn't the importance of that hard-earned remuneration worthy of your best care?

Money is important. People are eager to learn endlessly about wine, the latest hand-held technology devices, and numerous other subjects that are not likely on the priority list, but, when it comes to learning about money, which changes lives, they have no time for it or interest in it. At the end of the day, when our true needs for food and shelter have been met, it is easy to relax and feel that all is well. Hopefully, all is well, but all may not remain well if learning about and paying attention to your financial resources is not somewhere on your priority list. Besides, the world could always be better, much better, with wise financial stewardship.

I have noticed that people tend to pay more attention to their money during bear markets, while, during bull markets, there is more neglect of financial assets. Bad times tend to get our attention because they trigger fears, which demand our utmost attention. It can seem easier to live with something we are avoiding, but we all know that doesn't work as well as dealing with reality and making a plan to get things back on track when needed. This is true for everything in our lives, whether it's money matters, relationships or addictions. The goal for successful wealth management, then, should be equal and consistent attention during both good and bad times.

A Very Part Time Job with Excellent Pay

Hopefully, you now fully realize that no one cares about your money more than you do. You also know why you would like to have money. With this awareness, you are ready to step into the role of a capable and successful money manager. Begin thinking of yourself as being in the business of money management, your money management. This may feel a little scary at first. Yes, it is yet another job, but it is a part-time one of the utmost importance. What could be better than a job that only requires an hour or two a month and has an enormous payoff? If you have a spouse that has been overseeing your money, become a co-manager. You can divide the tasks but share the overall goals and responsibilities. What is required of this position?

- a commitment to your job

- adequate education

- staying current

- measurable goals to monitor and evaluate performance

Summary

We all pay attention to the things we care about. No one cares about your money more than you do. Learn what you need to know to manage it, and then pay attention to it, so that you can create the rich life that you want.

LIFE STORY

Jeanette felt that she had been fortunate. She married Brad, a man with a successful business and accumulated wealth (she thought). After the birth of her first child, she decided to stay home and raise him. She eventually had four children. Raising the children and managing their two homes left little time to be involved with monitoring their money. She completely trusted Brad with managing this aspect of their lives, and felt there would be plenty of time to get involved with their wealth management once the children were grown.

Brad came home from work early one afternoon while the children were still in school to let Jeanette know that he had lost his business due to competition. He had been gradually draining the family savings for years in order to keep the business afloat. They had $20,000 left in the bank, which would cover most of the current month's living expenses of $25,000. He had borrowed heavily against both homes. (Jeanette recalled signing the loan documents without getting the details.) When she asked Brad why he had not told her sooner, he said that he thought he could save the business, and that he hadn't wanted to upset her.

Financial Woman Steps

Define three areas of your life where you currently manage, or, in the past, have capably managed projects while knowing only one percent about the topic.

List the five most important things in your life.

Which of the five important things do you feel needs more focus from you?

CHAPTER FOURTEEN

KNOW WHERE YOUR MONEY IS

Don't link money to your emotions; when you do, it gives the power to your money, instead of giving you power over your money.

— Anne McKevitt
Globally recognized business leader,
Best Selling Author, TV personality, Philanthropist,
Member of President Bill Clinton's Clinton Global Initiative

This can seem almost too simple to suggest as a major principle of good wealth leadership, but, if you are someone who is committed to maximizing the growth of your money, then knowing where you are invested can actually be more in depth than it initially sounds. Some women have told me that they feel financially insecure because, even though they have been told where their money is invested, it seems like it is just out there somewhere in an unknown place. They don't feel the security that comes with knowing how to access their money, like they could at their local bank. I think this comes from not understanding the basics of the products in which they have invested. Lack of knowledge creates uncertainty; uncertainty creates doubt; doubt creates fear; and fear remains and is toxic for wellness.

RICH HABITS

Knowing the basics about where your money is invested empowers you, and that empowerment gives you financial confidence and peace of mind.

You have created your Own and Owe Statement that allows you to see how much money you have. This should immediately give you a sense of empowerment. Next, knowing where your money is means understanding the basics about each item listed in the "Own" section of that statement. As you begin to grow and invest your money, this exciting step requires new knowledge to feel confident and informed. This knowledge will empower you to make good decisions so that you can protect and successfully grow your capital.

If you are not yet to the point where you have enough money to begin investing, I still encourage you to read this chapter. I invite you to start thinking about the time in your life when you will have money to invest. This mindset will help you get there sooner. Develop good beliefs around growing your money. Start becoming prepared for this exciting phase in life now.

Do You Really Know Where Your Money Is?

It is important for anyone who has money in any stock or bond fund to know the basics about the type of asset owned. Just as you would never buy a refrigerator without first checking into the details beyond the price and the color, you should never buy an investment without knowing and understanding the basics of that investment. Knowing and understanding the basic information about any investment you have is the only way to really "know where your money is."

Knowing the basics about where your money is invested empowers you, and empowerment gives you confidence and peace of mind around your money. The basics of understanding any investment include knowing exactly what the asset is, who is managing it, and its risks, costs, time factors and performance numbers. The good news is that once you know the basics, you can use this knowledge to understand most other investments you own or will buy in the future.

Let's look at an example of applying "information savvy" to your money. Maybe you have chosen an investment option as a part of your 401K, or someone else, such as an advisor or a spouse, has chosen an investment in foreign stocks for your money. You know that you are invested in the foreign stock market, but here are some basics that you would want to know about that investment:

- Are you invested through a global or international fund?

- Is the fund invested in emerging or established markets?

- Are you just invested in a country or a region through an index fund, or maybe an ETF?

- Are the stocks invested in small companies or large companies?

- Are they chosen based on value or growth principles?

- Was fundamental or technical analysis used, or both?

- Do you own stocks through a private money manager, a hedge fund, a mutual fund, a limited partnership, or another type of structure?

- Is there some type of currency hedging used to reduce risk or capitalize on currency moves?

- Are there any strategies used to limit your risk in the event of a major market correction or extended bear market?

- What would be the best way to evaluate the performance of this particular investment?

I don't write these questions to overwhelm you with information, but these are the basics of any traditional investment. While the lingo and topics may sound intimidating, most of this information is intuitive and simple once you hear it.

For example, currency hedging sounds pretty daunting, but you don't need to learn how to hedge currency risk. Knowing, however, if you are protected from currency risk makes sense because it protects your capital. This knowledge gives you financial security. Similarly, a global fund refers to funds that invest in the U.S., while international funds do not hold companies in the U.S. This knowledge allows you to know how much of your money is invested outside of the U.S. Last, everyone needs to know the best way to evaluate the performance of ANY investment they own. You can see how simple and basic this information is.

Knowledge Empowers You To lead Your Team

While you don't need to know all the details of each company you own, the points above are the big picture attributes of your investments. The individual companies within funds are smaller details, for example. Again, the good news is that these same attributes apply to most investments, and, by learning these few basics, you will have information that will serve you well for life. Fortunately, the foundations of investing are not like technology, changing every year, thus creating a constant struggle to remain informed and current. The important thing is that by knowing this information, you really know where your money is.

Think of the difference between knowing that your money is in foreign stocks, and knowing that your money is invested with a private money advisor, who specializes in buying the stocks of undervalued large companies in developed countries and uses hedging to reduce currency risk. Furthermore, you know that this advisor invests a relatively small total amount of money, such as four billion dollars, and he has been investing internationally for ten years, with results that have been better than most foreign investors, with less risk. You know that he has the ability to have high amounts of cash, so that he can sell and take profits (for you) when the international large company stock market seems over valued or a crisis appears on the horizon. Also, you know that a stock will be sold if it has a twelve percent loss to limit your risk.

Now, you know where your money is. You did not need to spend hours and hours each month learning the details about what companies you own for every fund or investment. Instead, you spent a few hours learning the basic investment principles, and those principles give you the information you need to oversee management of your wealth, to lead your team. You'll be able to have meaningful conversations and ask the right questions of anyone involved with your money when you know these few basics. These same principles apply, for the most part, to mutual funds, hedge funds, retirement account options and privately-managed accounts. Think of how much better you will be with choosing financial professionals or investment products when you know this basic information!

 *Financial Woman Extra*

To receive a free handout of the basics you want
to know about any investment you own, go to:
FinancialWoman.com/tools

Expand Your Own and Owe Statement

From a more tactical standpoint, knowing where your money is also ties back to having order around your money, so you then know how much money you have and where your money is. You can now incorporate how and where your money is invested onto your Own and Owe Statement to go beyond the very basic information of only a dollar amount. Having this additional clarity about exactly where your money is will help you feel more confident about your money because knowledge lends confidence and security.

Studies show that many women have said that they really want to focus on financial security and the end results of managing their money well, such as sending their children to college or making a meaningful donation. This is the starting point rather than the ending point. These are your money reasons that you clarified earlier. Saying that you want to achieve your money reasons, or the end results, without having to learn the basics about managing your finances and investing your money is a little like saying, "I want to lose ten pounds, but I don't want to work out or eat differently." It is just not going to happen.

Summary

Anything worth doing requires effort, and, if your money and your money reasons are important to you, then you'll make the effort. It all comes down to a decision, as do most things in life. When you truly decide, you commit. When you commit, as a woman you can do things much, much more difficult than learning a few concepts that will empower you to grow your money. After all, many of us birth babies and raise children, including teenagers, and we survive to talk about how much we loved it! Surely, then, we can confidently and capably oversee our investments so that we can reach our financial goals.

LIFE STORY

Anita's husband, Joe, was great about managing their money. The two of them reviewed their finances and investments together occasionally, but sometimes it was unpleasant. Anita never felt that she truly understood the different investments they held in stocks, bonds, and commodities. She wasn't sure Joe knew the basic facts, either. She was confused about the risk levels and various factors associated with each investment. While she valued her husband's time commitment to monitoring their money, she wanted to be better informed so she could feel more capable. Anita took an investment course to help her better understand the basics of each of their investments. She felt more financially secure with the knowledge she gained.

Financial Woman Steps

On your Own and Owe Statement, list the major category of any investment you have if it is not already on your statement.

Add the name of the institution where the account is held, such as the brokerage firm or bank.

Add the facts you know about each investment. For example, for stock funds, indicate whether they are foreign or global funds, and whether they hold large or small companies. For a bond fund, you can add the duration of the bonds, such as short-term or long-term.

CHAPTER FIFTEEN

DELIBERATELY CHOOSE WHO WILL MANAGE YOUR MONEY

Don't relinquish your say in financial matters in order to avoid bruised egos. If you do, you'll only lengthen the time it takes you to become financially free.

— Lois Frankel, PhD
President of Corporate Coaching International,
International Best Selling Author, Speaker, TV Personality

Once you have enough capital to begin investing, one of the core wealth management decisions you'll make is whether to manage your own money or to hire someone to manage it for you. This should be a deliberate decision based on facts, not a default decision because there is a financial advisor or stock broker in the family or a close family friend. The step for reaching a decision about your investment management is twofold. First, ask yourself whether you want to invest your own money. If the answer is yes, then learn what you need to know in order to manage your money with the same or better results as a paid advisor or fund manager. If this seems

RICH HABITS

Always be aware that your primary investment objective is to make the highest return on your money after fees and taxes within your acceptable risk level.

impossible, know that this is done by many investors every day. If the answer is that you want to outsource the management of your wealth, learn what your options are based on your level of wealth. The amount of money you have to invest will determine the options you have for products and service providers. Then interview several potential candidates, and make a choice, or several, based on the strategy you have chosen.

Growing Your Money Is a Journey

Be aware that you can always change whatever decision you make about who will invest your money, but there may be costs related to taxes as well as transaction costs if there is a change later. Investing, however, is a learning process; you'll learn more as you go. Often knowledge brings an awareness of better methods to invest money. Don't stay with a product or service that is not serving you well just because of the hassle and expenses associated with making a change, as often happens. Sometimes, with investing, like everything else in life, you have to bite the bullet and make changes, even though it may be inconvenient or costly in the near term.

Your investment product and service options will also change as you accumulate more wealth. You'll learn about your skills as they relate to your money. You'll become more aware of investing options and strategies as your knowledge and portfolio grow, simply from being more involved. Investing is an ongoing process, also, because your investment objectives change as life changes. There are periods when you focus on growing your money and other times when you focus on income generation. These are referred to as investment objectives.

Markets change and evolve. As stated earlier, investing fundamentals mostly remain the same, but new financial products and services gradually come to market. Services and funds of all types are available for individual investors as well as financial advisors that no one would have imagined thirty years ago. Technology has also allowed technical analysis to enter into the equation. The use of derivatives, such as options, has increased significantly for investment products over the past few years in an effort to enhance performance and manage risk.

Some Questions to Guide You

If you are unsure whether or not you should use an advisor to manage your overall portfolio, or at least some of your portfolio, give some thought to the following questions to help you arrive at the best decision for you. If you already work with a financial advisor, these questions will help you clarify the role that your advisor plays.

- Are you interested in the topic of investing? We all tend to do a better job with the things we are interested in and enjoy. Keep in mind, however, that there will probably be aspects of investing that do not interest you, but you'll need to do them anyway. For me, that includes filing and bookkeeping.

- Do you have the time to research investments? Keep in mind that a simple strategy, such as a portfolio of index funds, takes very little time.

⟨⟨⟩ *Financial Woman Extra* ⟨⟩⟩

(For a free handout on index investing go to: **FinancialWoman.com/tools**)

Also, everyone's plate tends to seem full, but are there wasted hours that you could spend on your portfolio if you choose?

- Will you actually spend the time required?

- Will you or a professional get the best results after fees? This is probably the most important question.

- Do you tend to be organized?

- Do you tend to be disciplined?

- Do you like to read and research?

- Do you tend to follow through on your plans?

- Is your life so incredibly full right now that the thought of adding one more job, however time-consuming, completely overwhelms you?

- Are control or fear issues keeping you from hiring someone to manage your money when your returns would be better if you did?

You may also want to consider managing a portion of your money and having someone invest a portion for you. There are numerous options available here. Knowledge of what those options are will help you make informed and proactive decisions to achieve your wealth goals. Take some time to consider carefully the best option for you and your money with your eye on the end results you want, which are the money reasons you defined.

If you should decide that you want to hire someone to manage all of your money, again, the options available to you will depend on the amount of wealth you want managed. The more wealth you want managed, the more options you have. This is due to the guidelines that the various financial professionals have established for their own firms, the type of client they want and the government regulations implemented based on the structure of their products and services.

Many financial professionals are affiliated with a large brokerage firm, while others are independent. There are numerous credentials, as well as areas of expertise, within each of these categories.

⟳ *Financial Woman Extra* ⟲

This large topic is beyond the scope of this book, but you can receive a free report at: **FinancialWoman.com/tools** on the various types of credentials for financial advisors.

Keep Your Primary Goal in Mind

One other important aspect of a relationship with an advisor is having an understanding of how the advisor charges and the amount she charges. This will be covered in more detail in another chapter. As with every type of business, it is important to consider expenses and fees in making wealth management decisions. Over time, the amount you spend on fees, compounded, can make a meaningful difference in your portfolio performance. On the other hand, it is also important not to put the cart before the horse. Just as with considering taxes, consider fees, but do not let them be your primary objective. Your primary objective is to make the highest return on your money after fees and taxes within your accepted risk level. Always remember this. When comparing investment choices, be sure look at returns after fees have been deducted to get a true comparison. The return on your investments after fees, expenses and taxes is what you keep.

Summary

Regardless of your decision to invest or outsource your wealth management, you'll still want to know the basic principles of investing. The major asset classes and simple performance measures are all areas that you'll need to know to measure and evaluate performance. It's that one percent every woman needs to know to confidently oversee her money. The choice is yours. Be sure to make it with accurate, unbiased information.

LIFE STORY

Marta had just over $500,000 in her investment account. She discovered that she was not on track to reach her financial goals, based on the returns she had gotten in the past, and the amount she was saving each year. She decided to hire a money coach to help her figure out the best course of action for her to take next. Over the past few years, she had chosen mutual funds herself based on research that she did at the library. She and the coach saw that while she was selecting funds with good performance, her own investment performance was poor because she was buying and selling the funds at the wrong time; she had become emotional in her decisions rather than objective. The coach assured her that this is a common mistake that individual investors make. After learning about the various types of financial professionals available for her level of wealth from her money coach, she interviewed three independent financial advisors who charged reasonable flat fees to manage investments. With guidance from the coach, she saw that one advisor seemed most aligned with her investment goals based on her skill set and performance results.

Financial Woman Steps

> Answer the questions posed earlier in this chapter to clarify whether you would get better results managing your own money or working with a financial advisor.

CHAPTER SIXTEEN

HIRE AN ADVISOR FOR THE RIGHT REASONS

If you're truly listening and looking, most people are revealing more than they realize. Through body language, voice tone, words, and subtext, they'll tell you everything you need to know.

— **Gail Evans**
International Best Selling Author, Radio Host,
International Speaker, Past Executive Vice President CNN

If you are currently using or want to start working with a financial advisor, you may feel uncertain about how to find a good one. I believe there are many good advisors. The most important thing is to choose an advisor for the right reasons. Learn the one percent you need to know, so that you can evaluate any advisor you are currently using or considering. You want to make good choices, showing leadership and deliberateness with your money decisions.

Again, you don't choose an advisor simply because he is a family member or friend. While this definitely adds to the trust factor, there are other reasons to hire an advisor. If a family member or friend is the right person based on the reasons that you should choose an advisor, then that may be great, or it may not. A problem could arise if and when you want to work with a different advisor and the family

RICH HABITS

When choosing a financial advisor, consider performance, products, fees, integrity and service.

member or friend is offended. Only you can decide what is right for you. I will say that anyone with your best interests in mind will want you to have the highest return within your acceptable risk levels at the lowest cost. Having said that, the most important reasons for choosing an advisor are performance, products, fees, integrity and service.

Service

One of the complaints I hear most often from women about male financial advisors is that they do not show respect towards them. The complaints and indications of this are subtle, but some of the more common ways include: setting up appointments with husbands without checking with the wife's schedule, not making eye contact with the woman, and assuming the woman doesn't know anything about investing. There are several aspects of service that should be considered, but I think one of the most important ones is respect. I have personally experienced a lack of respect shown towards me as the woman in the relationship, even when I established the relationship. Women have shared with me numerous examples similar to the ones above; one client was actually told by her advisor that she was stupid. If you choose to continue paying an advisor who does not treat you with respect, you are voluntarily remaining in a place of financial disempowerment. Make a decision to work only with financial professionals who treat you with respect.

In addition to the personal relationship you have with an advisor, find out about the more tangible aspects of their service. Make sure that the services will work for you. Some good questions to ask include:

- What type of reports are issued? Look to see if you understand them; if not, ask if the reports can be provided in other formats.

- Do they host annual meetings or other events? If so, where and when, approximately, are they held?

- Do they have electronic newsletters or videos for clients?

- Will the advisor or a customer service representative be meeting with you?

- How often will you receive account updates, and how will they be delivered?

- Will tax saving strategies be implemented on your behalf?

Integrity

Since performance doesn't matter if all of your money is lost, integrity naturally resides at the top of the list of reasons to hire a particular advisor. While it seems as though this would go without saying, thousands of investors thought

Bernard Madoff had integrity, or they would not have invested with him. Credentials and certifications tell you about a financial professional's training, education and affiliations, but they do not necessarily ensure integrity. Don't assume that your friends or family know for certain, either.

Some basic steps to help verify integrity are:

- Checking into the accounting firm that handles an advisor's audits

- Knowing how long the accounting firm has been handling the advisor's account

- Checking into any major changes that have been made within the accounting firm in recent years

- Making sure the audit is independent

- Checking the advisor's history at Financial Industry Regulatory Authority's (FINRA's) website, http://www.finra.org/Investors/ToolsCalculators/BrokerCheck/

Products

The products and services offered by an advisor is a good starting point for making your selection. If a firm or advisor doesn't have the type of products you want, you can quickly move to your next possible choice. Advisor's offerings will depend on their area of expertise and also on the level of their client's wealth. Areas of expertise can include any of the following:

- Financial planning, including budgeting, tax and estate issues

- Individual security selection

- Choosing funds for clients, either large institutional accounts (more common) or mutual funds

Understanding how the amount of money you are seeking to have managed guides you to the right advisor is important. For example, if you have $100,000 to invest, then you may want to look for an advisor who places client's money into mutual funds or Exchange Traded Funds (ETFs) and also offers some financial planning. Due to changes in the ability of both individual investors and advisors to access money managers who previously required a minimum of $500,000 and more, many more products are now available to investors with lower amounts to invest. This new access applies to those who work with financial advisors and those who invest their own money.

If you have $2,000,000 to invest, you may want to interview advisors who specialize in choosing privately managed funds for their clients, or interview several advisors in different areas of expertise in individual security selection, such as a stock specialist or a bond specialist. You will probably also want a separate financial planning specialist to help with tax and estate planning strategies. By finding out the client net worth of the majority of an advisor's practice, you'll find out her product and service expertise, since certain products cater to different wealth levels. You also don't want to be the only client with

$2,000,000 invested with an advisor when all of the other clients have invested funds under $200,000. Likewise, if you have a $100,000 portfolio, you don't want to be the only client with under $4,000,000 at the firm.

Fees

Fees are discussed in another chapter, but they must be mentioned as an important reason for choosing or not choosing an advisor. If products with up-front load fees of three percent are common recommendations from one advisor, this must be considered when comparing this advisor to one that typically recommends products with no load fees. Again, while cost is not the bottom line, it is certainly a part of the equation in your investment returns, as it is with most aspects of life. Always ask the total amount of fees and expenses you will be incurring for your money management.

Performance

The best is for last: performance. Make sure you review and understand the performance for any fund or advisor you are evaluating. If you are considering hiring an advisor that outsources the management of your money, you can ask for the performance of the five funds she has placed most of her clients in over the past five or ten years. I like to get for performance numbers since inception. Be aware that the performance of the overall markets during various time frames is a large part of the equation related to performance. Ask any questions that you need to ask in order to understand the performance numbers, and be comfortable with the answers you receive.

I like to look at annual performance to see how investments have performed each year, not just three, five, or ten years lumped together and annualized. By looking at each year's performance, it's easy to see how the performance correlates with both up and down markets and the fluctuations that occur each year. While there are some useful risk comparison indicators, such as standard deviation, alpha and beta, looking at simple annual performance numbers is an easy way to see how an investment performs.

Summary

While recommendations from friends can be helpful, know enough to make good decisions about the financial professionals you choose. Sometimes, even well intentioned people don't know enough to know what they don't know, or they won't admit that they don't know. You want to make sure that whoever you chose for this important role is a good fit for both your investment needs and your personality.

LIFE STORY

Meredith decided that she was ready to begin using a financial advisor since her wealth had grown to over $500,000. After learning about the various types of financial professionals available for her level of wealth, she decided to interview three financial advisors. The third advisor she interviewed was the most accommodating in providing the returns that he had gotten for his clients. He showed her the funds that he had placed most of his clients in over the past nine years. While the initial information that he gave her on the funds had the typical performance data averaged over several years, he gladly showed her the annual performance upon request. He also provided several tools that measured the risk related to each fund, and took the time to explain each one. What she liked most of all was that he showed her how the performance of each fund compared to that of the related benchmark, after all expenses had been considered. Additionally, he suggested that she invest a portion of her money in a low cost commodity exchange traded fund that he would carefully monitor.

Financial Woman Steps

If you are currently working with a financial professional or a mutual fund company, how do you rate each of these areas?

Service
Integrity
Products
Fees
Performance

CHAPTER SEVENTEEN

CHOOSE YOUR VILLAGE WISELY

Know what you are not good at and delegate it.

— **Julie Clark**
Founder of Baby Einstein

O nce you are ready to invest a fairly large amount of money, you may wonder if you want to invest in more traditional investments, such as stocks and bonds, or invest in alternative investments. One important factor in this decision is the level of complexity you want your finances to have. Also, consider the amount of time you want to spend on your investments. There may be times in your life that allow for a significant amount of time to be spent on your investment pursuits, while other periods demand that you keep the time required at an absolute minimum. The higher your income, the more you may want to consider more alternative investments due to the tax advantages that many have. Be aware that alternative investments, such as real estate rentals and small business ownership, come with the need for additional support.

RICH HABITS

If you know you want to limit the number of people that are involved with your finances, your investment choices will be driven by this factor.

Decide What You Want, Then Invest

Some financial support is essential for most people; almost everyone needs a banker, and I suggest hiring a CPA as soon as possible. Most homeowners work with real estate brokers. Decide what you want, and then decide how to invest. For example, if you want simplicity and you really want to limit yourself to working with only two people, you probably don't want to get into real estate rental properties. This involves Real Estate Brokers, and possibly a Mortgage Broker, at least for a one-time occurrence. You'll also need a real estate management company, unless this is your area of expertise or you want to self-manage the properties, but even this will likely require some maintenance support. Your taxes will be more complicated, and you will also need some legal work done for your real estate holdings. Real estate investments can have huge rewards, but may not be as passive as they seem.

You may decide that you want to keep things really simple, so that you can avoid having to involve any more support team than you absolutely must. In this case, the minimum will probably include a CPA, depending on the level of your wealth, and some type of money manager.

Even if you choose and manage your own index funds with a small amount of money, there will be a fund management company or brokerage firm that will hold the funds and provide custodial service, although your time involvement will be very minimal.

Several years ago I was a participant in a year-long, very intensive financial training program promoting alternative investments. While I learned a great deal of helpful information, I was not aware of the complexity involved in managing some alternative investments, such as rental real estate partnerships, limited partnerships, angel investing, and small oil and gas trusts. There are simple ways to invest in more traditional alternative investments. For example, you can invest in real estate through Real Estate Investment Trusts (REITs); you can invest in oil and gas exploration through publicly-owned limited partnerships that provide excellent and timely documentation that you'll need for accounting purposes; or you can easily buy low cost index or ETFs for commodity investments. Smaller, alternative investments are often unable to fund support staff for documentation for their investors, and factors are frequently more complicated than anticipated with private funding and angel investing. Tax preparation fees will also be higher for investors with more complex portfolios. The upside to this inconvenience is that there is frequently significant tax benefits associated with alternative investments.

All of this isn't to say that if you have a knack for real estate or angel investing that you shouldn't pursue this type of investment. More complex investments frequently provide the opportunity for higher returns. You may, however, want to limit the type of alternative investments to only one to two to reduce complexity. Now, let's look at a few of the various team members that you may want in your village.

Banker/Lender

It's important for everyone to have a relationship with a person at a bank. Take out a loan for a small amount at a time when you don't need it in your own name; the only time you can borrow easily is when you don't need a loan. Establish a line of credit, also when you don't need it, so that it will be there if and when you do. You may decide to start your own business or buy an existing one. If you do, your line of credit can provide funds for starting your business. You may even be able to lock in a low interest rate as an extra benefit, depending on the interest rate cycle.

Brokerage Company

Your broker and banker may be at the same company since many former banks and brokerage firms have merged. You will use a brokerage firm to buy and sell securities such as stocks, bonds and many types of funds. If you use a financial advisor or money manager to invest for you, then she will have one or more brokerage firms she uses for buying and selling securities for her clients.

Bookkeeper

As previously mentioned, I support the theory that, if something isn't getting done, the reason doesn't matter as much as the fact that it is not getting done. Consider hiring a bookkeeper if your books are not done in an orderly way. This is probably not an issue until you have some degree of complexity in your finances, such as multiple investment accounts, or alternative investments, such as real estate rentals or small business ownership. Once your finances become complicated, hire a bookkeeper if you're not able to develop a clear and easy system that will enable you to stay on top of your money. Depending on where you live, it's likely that you can find someone locally on Craigslist®. Elance® and Guru® are also great places to hire someone virtually. If this makes you nervous, your CPA firm can probably recommend someone because it makes their job easier when your records are organized. Once you establish a level of trust with this person, she can easily download the information she needs to prepare your reports. This will make your job of being the CEO of your money much easier.

CPA

A good CPA should be on your wealth management team as soon as the budget allows for tax planning and preparing your returns. If your CPA is good, it is likely that she will pay for herself in the first year. The most common designation for accountants in the United States is from the American Institute of Certified Public Accountants (AICPA). The designation indicates that they have passed an exam given by the AICPA and have the related experience.

Interview CPAs to find one that suits your needs. Here are a few questions to ask if you are interviewing an accountant. If you already have a CPA, these questions should help you improve your working relationship with her.

- Will you send me reminders to get my documentation to you, and what are the expectations for your time frame?

- Do you prepare my quarterly returns, if necessary?

- Will you be making suggestions for tax saving strategies specifically for my situation?

- Do you have an area of expertise that applies to most of your clients, such as real estate, stock trading, active investing and small business entities? If you are seeking a CPA who specializes in a specific area, then ask what percentage of her clients are engaged in the specific area.

- Do you update your clients when IRS rules change that will affect their taxes during the year?

- Who will actually prepare the return, and what are her credentials?

- Will you be able to personally speak with the CPA when necessary? If not, then who will be your contact person?

- Do you file electronically?

- How often do you suggest meeting with your clients?

- How do you charge for your meeting time?

- How do you charge for return preparation?

- Do you send publish a newsletter for your clients? If so, request a copy.

- What type of client has not fit well into your practice in the past?

- What are the long-term plans for the firm?

The last question is important because there could be plans to sell the firm on the horizon. I learned this lesson the hard way: After researching and interviewing three firms, I finally decided on one. Unfortunately, immediately after I began working with my accountant there, he sold the practice. It was annoying, but probably not unethical for him not to tell me during the interview process that the firm was about to be sold.

I have found that the longer you have a good relationship with a CPA, the better. When returns are prepared, old returns may need to be accessed. If you have been with the same CPA for a long time, she will have the old documents in her office. If not, you will most likely be the one pulling and faxing or scanning old returns and information. In the end, it will save you time because your CPA will get to know your investments and your patterns of living, which affect your returns (i.e. charitable giving, medical expenses, dependents and entities).

If you have an area that requires more expertise, such as owning your own business through one or more entities, real estate rentals or stock trading, and you cannot find a CPA in your home area with that particular expertise, I suggest considering someone outside of your area. Because it's easy to transfer data now, there is no reason that you need to be in the same town. Most business is conducted over the phone, anyway. I have been told by a CPA that the occurrence of audits decreases with an out-of-state CPA, although I personally do not have the numbers to support that claim. The main point is to find someone who really knows the area in which you require expertise. For most investors, a good broad-based, local CPA should be fine.

It is not always easy to find a CPA who really delves into your finances and suggests tax-saving strategies. It is always easier to do a job basically the same for all clients, but what you want to find is someone who will really work with you and your specific needs and issues. I suggest that you get a couple of referrals from any CPA you consider; keep in mind that you are going to get the names of some of the happiest clients. Call them and ask if the CPA recommended ideas for lowering taxes based on their financial situation.

Another significant consideration is timing. You know whether or not you are organized and proactive enough to have your documents to your CPA on February 15 without any prodding, or if you will need someone who reminds you and is patient. If you are not the organized and proactive person that you long to be, then let anyone you are considering to hire know this. I know I need a CPA who will be patient with me when I don't have this at the very top of my priority list in January. Also, if you become involved with investments in small partnerships and various types of entities, tax documentation often arrives last minute. This frequently requires requesting an extension for filing your return.

Make sure that you find out what kind of schedule the CPA has to be sure that it is a good fit for your needs. Does he have so many clients that one kink in the schedule will delay your filing, or does he have plenty of staff to handle the inevitable delays that happen every April and October? Clarify this, so that you can find a firm that works for your schedule and personality.

Even though you won't be marrying your CPA, hopefully you are going to have a very long term and financially-rewarding relationship with her. Choose someone with whom you will look forward to brainstorming tax saving ideas and strategies. This will be one of the most important relationships in your village.

Estate Attorney or Financial Planner

An estate attorney or a financial planner can help you plan the best legal and tax strategies for your money. This person can help you make sure that you have the right amount of money in the most advantageous accounts, and that all legal documents are in place. Examples of this would include issues like:

- Making sure your children, who may have just reached the legal age of adulthood (it varies by state), cannot legally get money that they are not yet ready to manage

- Establishing a living trust that allows you to avoid probate and easily manage assets when a family member dies

- Structuring a trust to reduce family taxes in the long-term when one spouse dies. This is a common legal and planning task

- Designating the best beneficiary

- Setting up accounts in the most tax-beneficial ways, such as tenants in common versus joint tenants with rights of survivorship

- Creating an entity for a small business

All of these issues are important, and the time to get them setup correctly is prior to dealing with the outcome of the decisions. Continually monitor, re-evaluate and modify all of your financial details as your wealth increases, life changes and legal and tax issues are modified.

Many of these details can be handled by a financial planner, while others will need an attorney. You can let your financial planner and estate attorney work as a team for you if you require services from each. The financial planner may cost less than the attorney, or you may already use a planner to help manage your investments. If this is the case, make sure you specifically address these details. It is amazing how often they slip through the cracks until it is too late. Death is never pleasant to anticipate, but it is going to happen to all of us at some point, so you may as well set up your wealth in the most beneficial way for your family. The thought of dying while knowing that this is still on the "to do" list is daunting. There is no time like the present; get your assets in order now.

Over the past few years, online legal documentation

firms have developed. While they are not able to offer specific legal advice, they have some excellent information if you would like to research and implement these details on your own. The forms from these firms are usually less expensive than having an attorney prepare the documents. This technique may make sense if you are not quite to the stage where an estate attorney would be necessary, but you know what strategies and documents you need to get in place. Remember, online document preparation cannot replace getting specific advice from your attorney.

Fund Manager or Private Money Manager

Whether you use a fund manager or private money manager depends on your level of wealth. There are many different types, with various roles and credentials. Know that they are a part of your team in some way if you are investing money, unless you are choosing your own stocks, bonds or other investments. They are part of your village, your team, and they are working for you because you are paying them. Do what you need to do to monitor the results. If you are working with a private money manager or wealth advisor, establish a relationship with her. Be educated, so that you can participate in meetings, ask questions, and demonstrate control over your money.

Money Coach

Money coaches have gained popularity over the past decade, especially when investors decided to take control of their money after incurring losses in the 2008 and 2009 financial crisis. Working with a money coach is an excellent way to:

- Gain the knowledge you need to invest

- Get unbiased information since they typically do not sell investment products or money management services

- Work through old money beliefs to establish your own beliefs

- Help reconcile your life goals to your money goals

- Explore ways of increasing income or decreasing spending

- Establish and maintain new, improved money habits

- Learn the financial professional options available for you and the typical costs based on your level of wealth

- Understand how to evaluate the performance results you are getting from an investment or financial professional

Money coaches don't necessarily have a certification but, rather, knowledge based on experience or a previous career. They typically cost less than the amount spent on a financial advisor and focus more on education or personal growth. Some money coaches teach a very specific skill, such as how build a simple low cost index fund portfolio or generate income with covered calls, while others may focus more on mindset. Fees vary, but group coaching programs or telecourses offered over the phone or via computer are usually a cost-effective way to get financial education. On the other hand, private coaching sessions can cover more specific or private needs but at a higher cost.

The best advantage of a coach is that she is usually not tied to promoting a specific product or service, so she is able to provide completely unbiased information. From that information, you can then make your own informed choices. (*Disclaimer:* I work as a money coach, providing financial and investment education to help clients create the life they want while becoming more financially secure.)

Mortgage Broker

I suggest that you ask a mortgage broker to give you a quote on the best rate when you are buying a house or taking out another large loan. This is more logical than asking only your bank and taking what they offer. Remember, you are the customer since you are paying them. As the borrower, you do pay for the broker, but only if you use her, which you will if she finds the best rate and terms for your mortgage. If she does, then she has probably saved you a significant amount of money. A small change in your rate can have a huge impact on your cost due to the time frame of a mortgage. This seems like a win to me.

Real Estate Broker

If you own a home, you have probably had a real estate broker on your team. You may not feel that a real estate broker should be considered a member of your wealth management village, but they are directly responsible for the purchase and sale of what may be your largest financial asset. You pay them a substantial amount of money, and anyone who receives payment for assisting you with your financial endeavours is a part of your village. You may decide to work with an agent because she is your friend, but you may have multiple friends who are agents. If this is the case, I suggest hiring the top-selling agent at a firm that specializes in your neighborhood. If you want to help your friends out, let them know that your house is going on the market, and they can, subsequently, bring their clients as buyers. This way, they can represent the buyer and still get half the commission.

Real Estate Management or Leasing

If you own rental properties, you may have real estate managers or leasing companies in your village. We use a leasing agent but handle the property management ourselves because we have a reliable maintenance person for our properties that we can call in case of an emergency. I won't go into the finer details since everyone reading this book will not be owners of rental real estate, but I will point out that the size of your village will expand if you own properties.

Relationships with Your Team

Working with your financial village is like any other job

that requires leadership and skill. It can take time to learn these skills and realize what is reasonable to expect in the way of customer service. As women, I think we tend to blame ourselves first when relationships end, sometimes even unpleasantly. When this happens, I always ask myself two questions:

1. What did I learn from this experience?

2. What could I have done differently?

I always learn something from my mistakes, but strained relationships take time and energy. This is why it is so important to converse as much as possible during the interview process. Selecting the right people the first time for your village alleviates wasted time and effort in the future. Terminating a relationship is difficult enough without the added pressure of transitioning to someone else. If a relationship begins to deteriorate, be proactive, but respectful, by clearly stating what your expectations were according to the notes you took during the interview, so that there is a chance to remedy the relationship before it becomes strained. If it fails nonetheless, take responsibility for your role in the scenario. You may not have trusted your gut in the hiring process, or you didn't do the necessary research in order to make a wise decision. Even so, you may just have to acknowledge that sometimes things don't work out as we had planned. Don't beat yourself up, just own that it didn't work, and then move forward. Know that you are now a better leader, probably in all areas of your life, as a result of what you have learned.

Summary

First choose the level of complexity you want in your investments based on the amount of time you have, the amount of money you are investing, and your tax situation. Determine the tasks that are associated with managing your money; decide which tasks you will handle, which tasks other family members will handle, and which tasks you will outsource. Then, select good members for your village that will provide the support you need to reach your financial goals.

LIFE STORY

Donna realized that she would need to get better returns on her investments than what she had gotten in the past in order to reach her financial goals. She realized, after analyzing her expenses, she was paying a lot of money in income taxes from the mutual fund she owned because it was incurring short term capital gains that were taxed at her highest tax rate. She took a course to learn about alternative investment strategies that had the potential to increase her returns while also providing some tax lowering benefits. She knew that she did not want to spend a lot of time on her investments since she worked full time and had a family. She decided to invest some of her portfolio in an oil and gas partnership since it didn't require an additional time commitment, had good potential for a 12% return, and provided tax benefits.

Financial Woman Steps

Make a list of the tasks involving your money management.

Write the name of the person who will do each task on the list.

Assign a time deadline for doing the task or for hiring the right person to do it.

Put the deadline on your calendar.

CHAPTER EIGHTEEN

KNOW HOW MUCH
YOUR MONEY COSTS YOU

Your portfolio, like your house, needs to reflect your personality.

— David M. Darst
Managing Director and Chief Investment Strategist
of Morgan Stanley

Would you join a health club that charges your bank account each month for the membership cost without first finding out how much you'll be billed? I think almost everyone would first find out how much the services cost and then make a decision about joining, based on that cost. The same can be said for phone service plans, checking accounts, sanitation services and child care. You would probably never consider any of these services without first investigating the cost (or at least I hope not). But, for some reason, many people either don't ask about the cost of their wealth management, or don't understand the different layers of expenses.

Beyond everyday banking and finance services, there are many types of financial professionals used for managing

RICH HABITS

It is important to understand how much you are spending on your wealth management, just as you do in other areas of your life.

money. The kind that you will choose depends mostly on your level of wealth and your specific investments, as mentioned in other chapters. Most of the information presented in this chapter applies to all different types of financial professionals, whether they are mutual fund managers, private money managers, or investment advisors that manage your overall portfolio. The same principles apply to almost any type of financial professional. Gain the ability to confidently monitor and evaluate the service and the investment results you are getting.

Fee Structures

There are various types of fee structures used in the financial services industry. Be sure that you understand how you pay anyone that you currently use or are considering using. Learn a few basics and gain the ability to monitor your investment costs with skill. Financial professionals usually get paid in the following ways:

- A percentage of the value of your assets that they manage

- An hourly fee for their time

- A set fee

- A commission on the securities they buy or sell

- A combination of the above

Many independent investment advisors are known as fee-only, meaning that they are paid only by the fees their clients pay them. On the other hand, a commission-based advisor will be paid a fee for selling products.

A commission-based advisor is often associated with a financial institution, such as a brokerage firm, bank or an insurance-based company. Most stock brokers work as commission-based professionals, but larger accounts may be handled as a "wrap account," meaning that a percent fee is charged. Ideally, if you have a lot of transactions, the firm representative that you deal with should let you know if the wrap structure would be less expensive than the commission structure. The term "fee-based advisor" is used for financial professionals who charge both commission sales and fees for service from their clients. It is always appropriate to ask the cost of anything, including your investments, if you don't know.

Hedge funds, which are available for high net worth investors, have fee structures that are a little more complicated. They usually involve a percent of the profits above a certain amount. In addition, a management fee is usually charged when investing in hedge funds.

As financial institutions continue to merge, the fee structures associated with each type of firm will change, and the old rules may no longer apply. The one rule that always applies, however, is to know what your investment expenses are. The way to know the cost of a service or product is to simply ask.

Part of being an empowered investor is being aware of the amount of your savings or capital that will be paying for your wealth management. Good service is nice, but investment performance results pay for the service and get you to your financial goals. The amount of time a financial professional is spending on your account is not as relevant as successful returns on your money.

There seems to be some shame or embarrassment associated with asking about wealth management costs. This may come from not feeling knowledgeable about how much you should be paying. Maybe it feels a little like asking someone how much money they make, a question deemed unforgiveable in our society.

Mutual Fund Fees

Fees associated mutual funds are sometimes much less apparent than the expenses associated with higher-end, private money management because you don't receive a statement of expenses. For this reason, I suggest seeking an expense ratio from an independent mutual fund service. This can easily be found at the library for free. Part of your job in monitoring your expenses is to know where and how to look for your investment costs.

Summary

If you want to feel empowered around your money, you must know how much it is costing you. You are probably doing this in every other area of your life. Once again, you can see how investing principles are just like other life principles, where you already feel confident and empowered. Your money should be at least as important as those other areas of your life.

LIFE STORY

Diana had never understood the fees associated with her financial advisor, Beverly. Because Diana had used Beverly's services for so many years, she felt awkward asking about the fee structure. This was compounded by the fact that the two had become friends over the years. Nevertheless, it bothered Diana, because she knew she would never pay for another service without first asking about the cost. Once she finally asked Beverly about her fee structure, she gladly explained it. Diana realized that this was an appropriate and legitimate question concerning their business relationship. She felt more confident knowing and understanding the cost of her wealth management.

Financial Woman Steps

Find out the range of expenses incurred with investment products and services similar to yours by taking a course or doing research.

Bring investing talk out of the closet; discuss investing and banking costs with your closer friends and family.

Just do it; ASK the person or company providing the service or product the cost issues addressed in this chapter.

CHAPTER NINETEEN

WHAT YOU EARN AFTER TAXES CAN GROW

Taxes are the number one cost in our lives. We know this. But for some reason we believe that the topic is either too boring or complex to be worth investing any time into. Hell, I felt the same way even after I was a CPA.

— **Mark J. Kohler, CPA**
Attorney at Law

Y ou know that investment expenses directly reduce the earnings from your investments. The other big hole in the bucket is income taxes. Both of these expenses can be difficult to see. Many believe it is wrong to try to pay as little as possible in income taxes. My belief is that it is smart to legitimately save as much as possible on taxes. This strategy leaves more money to manage and grow, which actually provides even more money to be given to the causes that you support. You can go to prison for income tax evasion. No amount of money is worth that! You can, however, be smart about your income taxes. This is what I encourage you to do.

RICH HABITS

Look over your previous year's tax return prior to meeting with your accountant. Ask her to explain what you do not understand, and how you can specifically save on your taxes for the upcoming year.

You Mean Income Taxes Are Not a Fixed Expense?

When you have some basic knowledge about the deductions that are allowed, you will begin to discover new ways to save on your income taxes. This is an ongoing process. It does not require a lot of time, but it needs some of your attention, especially if your income varies from year to year. Remember, income taxes are an expense in your monthly cash flow calculation. They definitely deserve attention because they may be your largest expense. Income taxes belong in the "Variable Expense" part of your Cash Flow Statement, not in the "Fixed Expense" section. What does this tell you? It tells you that they can usually be reduced or increased, based on the steps you do or do not take.

Aside from acquiring some minimal knowledge about expenses you can legitimately deduct, I suggest hiring an outstanding CPA with whom you meet at least once a year (not just in March to hand over your paperwork, because it's too late then to plan for the prior year). My suggestion is to do a little research, get some ideas together and meet with your CPA in late April, while you have your taxes fresh on your mind. You'll still have time to implement tax reduction strategies for the year. This makes sense because there is simply no way that your CPA can know all of the activities in the lives of every client.

Look over your previous year's tax return prior to the meeting with your accountant. This is a great way to understand the system, because you are already familiar with your habits and your own numbers. Ask your CPA to explain what you do not understand. Ask specifically how to save for the upcoming year based on the previous year's return and discuss any new strategies she suggests. Find a CPA who answers this question with some significant suggestions. There are a lot of CPA's, and while many are not proactive in helping you find ways to reduce your income taxes, there are some who are.

It's important to know your estimated income before meeting with your CPA because it can affect whether or not a deduction or claiming a loss is advantageous or allowed. To have a good idea of what both your income and capital gains and losses will be for the year, I suggest keeping a simple spreadsheet with non-recurring items and major deductible expenses. If you have a major taxable event, such as the selling of a property, an IRA transfer from a regular to a Roth IRA, or any taxable event of significance, put it in your spreadsheet so that you can easily know what your expected income is for the year (special rules may apply). This will only take a few minutes, but it will be a useful planning tool throughout the year. As a general rule, you can use the previous year's income as a guide for your current income unless your income is unpredictable from year to year (all the more reason to strategize).

The three areas related to income taxes that you want to make sure you are covering are:

- Utilizing deductions to the fullest

- Placing investments in the most tax advantaged account types

- Analyzing the creation of a small business to generate income while lowering taxes

Utilizing deductions to the fullest

You'll want to have some knowledge in this area so that you know what information to track and provide your CPA. Even small and easy tactics can make a difference in your tax bill. For example, consider prepaying or delaying property taxes on your home. Also, consider the timing of charitable deductions. Find out if you usually itemize deductions, and ask for a list of items that qualify to be itemized. Again, the impact of this will vary depending on your specific situation, so check with your CPA.

Placing investments in the most tax advantaged account types

This is the easiest way to reduce your taxes. Beyond making sure that you fully take advantage of legitimate write-offs, placing your investments into the most tax advantaged account provides an opportunity to grow more of your money. Let's look at a simple example of an account with the following details:

Account size-$100,000

Investment Return-8%

Additional Annual Amount Added to the Account-
$10,000

Federal Tax Rate-28%

State Tax Rate-6%

Using the above data, this $100,000 investment
would grow to $321,478 over a 10-year period in a taxable
account. In a tax-deferred account, that same amount
would grow to $ 682,236. The difference is astounding!
It's important to note that many investment returns have
more favorable tax rates than those used in this example,
but this demonstrates the difference for an account taxed
at an ordinary tax rate.

Creating a small business to increase earnings while lowering taxes

While this strategy takes more time and involves
additional expenses, as previously covered, the savings
can be more substantial. This is particularly effective with
the creation of an entity for your small business. This tax
reduction strategy is one of the major benefits of moving
from employee to consultant status with your career, as
mentioned in an earlier chapter. If you are considering this
plan, I suggest you find a CPA who specializes in this area.

Summary

Develop a tax-saving mindset. Know the percent for your highest tax rate and consider it when making decisions that may have tax implications. Funds to pay income taxes are paid right out of either your earnings or your investment capital. The more that is paid in taxes, the less you have to grow and compound.

LIFE STORY

Karen was in the thirty-three percent federal income tax bracket. Fortunately, due to reading a book about simple tax saving ideas, she realized that a $10,000 expense she had incurred qualified to be taken against ordinary income. That simple realization saved Karen $ 3,300 at tax time. She gave half of the tax savings as a contribution to a women's shelter, and put the other half back into her business for marketing so she could grow her company.

Financial Woman Steps

Look over last year's tax return.

Research online or ask your CPA about items you do not understand.

Read a simple book on income taxes, and note ways that you can legitimately reduce your taxes.

CHAPTER TWENTY

CHOOSE A METHOD TO STAY INFORMED

Pain is the messenger that is trying to tell us to learn something and change.

— Lorin Beller Blake
Founder Big Fish Nation, Author, Speaker

You know how you just know not to wear pleated, baggy pants when flat front, straight-leg pants are in style? It is almost like an intuitive knowledge, but it's not intuitive; you just know. You know what is in style by simply paying attention, by flipping through your regular magazines and noticing the styles and by watching movies or TV. All of the images trigger ideas and thoughts that you act on as you shop and dress. That awareness is what we are aiming for in the world of your finances and investing. Your new money savvy will affect your daily spending and earning habits, and also your mindset. There are several easy ways to incorporate this awareness into your life without having to spend a lot of time on it.

RICH HABITS

Once you establish a routine with a brief but regular form of financial media, it becomes something that you enjoy; you begin to feel confident and empowered with your knowledge about what is happening in the financial world.

Notice money happenings going on all around you

You are already naturally doing some of this simply by being a consumer. Examples include: dealing with interest rates on your mortgage or credit cards, noticing employment trends and hearing about them on the news, and recognizing inflation or deflation from changing prices while shopping. The platinum necklace you've wanted for years has suddenly increased significantly in price, and your favourite retailer has more clearance clothes than regular-priced items. It costs three times as much to fill your car as it did only one year earlier, or the cost of some types of food has doubled. Each of these observations provides valuable information about economic cycles (interest rates, inventory levels, employment trends) or commodity prices (oil, metals, coffee, corn); the two are generally intertwined. Simply paying attention will help you recognize over-exuberance in any type of market; this is a precursor to market corrections that can significantly affect the value of your investments.

Don't worry, I am not suggesting you become a commodity trader, but I would love to help you feel prepared to become a more informed investor. The goal is to grow your money; the more informed you are about how the financial markets are affected by the economy, the better; you can easily incorporate this information and knowledge into your world with just a little time and energy.

Get plugged into at least one regular media source

Propel your knowledge by choosing one or two media sources, so that you can stay connected to what is happening in the financial world. This will expand both your comfort level and your wealth mindset. Commit to spending a few minutes a week reading, listening to, or watching information about the economy and the markets.

With all of the new technology available, lack of time is no longer a valid excuse for not being informed about the financial world. Everyone can find a few minutes to listen to the financial news while commuting, working out or running errands. Choose a method that you will actually use to stay updated on broad economic and market trends. It should be based on your strongest skill set, personal preferences, schedule and technical expertise. You may prefer reading. I love reading with a highlighter in hand, but I also listen to recordings on my phone almost daily to fully utilize my time and expand my mind. You may also prefer an application on your hand-held device. Reading a publication or listening to a downloaded audio each fall at different ends of the spectrum.

I use a combination of old-fashioned publication reading, listening to the business news while making my morning tea, and a couple of online newsletters sent via email. This feels comfortable to me. It requires five to ten minutes a day to stay informed about what is going on in the financial markets and to remain aware of larger trends. I simply like knowing when the stock market has returned to near an eighteen-month high, or that commodity stocks have been strongly increasing in value for six months. Half an hour a week is all it takes to read a good weekly publication; this would also do the job. I actually look forward to curling up with my financial newspaper during the weekend, which I have delivered to my house to make it happen. Develop a routine with whatever works for you and your schedule.

Start having money conversations

Once you develop a money mindset and start paying attention to economic clues, you'll naturally begin feeling more knowledgeable about money. It is that simple. Pay attention. Increase your awareness. Then you'll become more comfortable with conversing about finances and investing. Talk about investing with like-minded friends or family; just be careful about taking advice. And be aware that everyone may not support you in your money journey. Having stated that, know that it's okay to talk about money. Money is good, not evil.

Avoid TMI (Too Much Information)

Whatever methods you choose to stay current, it's important that you don't take in too much information. This can lead to "analysis paralysis." Choose two or three information sources at the most, and stick to them. Start with one for a few weeks, and then you can add another source once your first habit is established. Pay more attention to facts and data than to predictions by "experts." The activity in the financial markets will actually tell you what is truly happening in those markets.

Summary

After you establish a few habits that will allow you to stay more current about the economy and the financial markets, this will become something that you enjoy. Once you see that this new routine can actually help you reach your financial goals sooner, you'll love it all the more. You will begin to feel the confidence and empowerment that come from being savvy about what is happening in the financial world. That empowerment is what will sail you to your financial goals through more conscious spending and better financial choices on a daily basis, which will provide more money for you to invest and grow.

Financial Woman Steps

What type of media could you easily fit into your life today to enhance your wealth mindset?

Do you want financial updates daily, weekly or monthly?

Do you want information delivered in a readable format, through television or online?

What source will you incorporate into your life now?

PART THREE

THROUGHOUT THE JOURNEY, ALWAYS GIVE

CHAPTER TWENTY-ONE

GIVE

Instead of "but", say "and".

— **Amilya Antonetti**
Award Winning Entrepreneur,
Best Selling Author, Media Personality

Now let's look at the third important element of creating a rich life: giving. You'll see that giving actually overlaps with the topics covered in the earning and growing sections of this book. There are three elements of giving that I'll address in this chapter. The first is the giving of your talents; the second is the giving of your time, and the third is the giving of your money.

Share Your Talents with the World

Everyone has a special gift to share with the world. In the chapter on increasing income, I pointed out that, due to the development of technology, it is easier than ever to create a small business through which you can share your talents with the world. Even though you're increasing your income, you're still sharing your gifts. When you share your

RICH HABITS

Share your time, your talents and your money to make a
difference in your life and the lives of others.

gifts, you are helping others in ways that they are seeking
to be helped in order to make their lives better; everyone
benefits. The money that you earn from sharing your gifts
then goes to help you accomplish your money reasons. This
is true whether you earn money from a salaried position, as
a professional or as a business owner.

Fortunately, there is an evolution in education focused
on using and growing your talents to support yourself.
When I went to college, the focus was being able to get
a job with enough salary to support myself. While this
is unquestionably an important factor, I also believe that
pursuing your passions, which usually relates to your natural
talents, is a consideration of at least equal importance. This
is true for several reasons.

Enjoyment Leads to Accomplishment

First, you are more likely to do what it takes to succeed
when you are doing something you enjoy. While success
has many definitions, for this purpose we'll define it as
being able to support yourself in a lifestyle and manner
that you enjoy, while also leading you to your life goals
(or your money reasons). When you are doing something
that is naturally pleasurable, you are much more likely to

spend the necessary time to create a fruitful endeavour. The enjoyment factor of working in an area based on your passion simply doesn't compare to the 8:00 to 5:00 cubicle job, where you are doing something you don't enjoy, just so you can pay the mortgage.

Talents Naturally Improve Results

When you are utilizing your natural talents and strengths, you are just more likely to excel in your work. Have you ever noticed how hard it is to do well with tasks that are outside of your natural talents? I saw this recently when my sons were in high school. They were required to succeed in areas that were outside of their strengths. I had forgotten how difficult this can be.

Life is full of tasks, of course, where we don't naturally excel. (Technology and housekeeping immediately come to mind!) We then become stronger in those areas that don't come naturally, but success is much sweeter when you are flowing in your natural abilities and passions. If you can spend the majority of your time doing passion based work, you are simply more likely to experience success in your life.

Enjoy the Process

You simply get to live a life that you enjoy when you are using and developing your talents through the work that you do. All the money in the world cannot diminish that important lifestyle consideration. If this seems like an impossible goal right now, you can work toward creating this existence. As I covered earlier in this book, life happens during the journey toward your money reasons; it's simply too short to spend most of your days doing something you don't enjoy. Of course, we frequently must do those things we don't enjoy in order to do the things we do enjoy, as I often remind my sons. However, if your work involves your natural abilities and passions, you will enjoy your days more. This is one of the keys to a rich life; it is about the giving of your best self.

Time

The second element of giving is your time. Countless charities need volunteers. You may not be able to give much of your money yet, but you still can give your valuable time and talent. If you have children or grandchildren, you can find volunteer opportunities that involve them. This is a wonderful way to model giving. If you can tie your giving into your natural talents, then it is all the more wonderful. You'll enjoy yourself doubly because you'll get that great feeling that comes from giving, while, at the same time, you'll be doing something that you love.

Giving Money

The third element of giving relates to giving your money. When you give to help others, it not only helps you, it helps the world. I believe this is important for several reasons.

- Giving fosters a habit that is based on sound principles of wealth and stewardship that have existed throughout history.

- You are almost certain to naturally become a more conscious spender when you give.

- Giving is good for your soul. It has been said that we give to help ourselves, not others, and I believe there is definitely an element of truth in this.

- Giving models an important sharing principle for the young people in your life.

- Financial contributions often provide tax benefits that allow you to have more money to give to the causes you support, which are based on your beliefs and ideals.

Summary

There is joy in giving. While giving helps others, it definitely helps us, as well. It has been said that this is the real reason we give. When we share our talents, time and money, with others, everyone wins.

Financial Woman Steps

Write down one gift that you would like to share in some capacity.

Define how you would like to share the gift you chose.

Write the action steps you'll take to implement your idea.

CHAPTER TWENTY-TWO

TAKING A NEW AND EMPOWERED JOURNEY

Successful people are willing to do what others aren't.

— Fabienne Fredrickson
Founder, ClientAttraction.com, Inc.
500/5000 fastest-growing companies

As you have seen throughout this book, good financial principles are very much like those we see in many other areas of our lives. Once again, we have another profound truth that applies to our financial journey, as well as other life experiences: the change takes place in the follow-up. You have clarified the life that you want; now go and create it. It's that simple.

A financial woman is someone who embraces her financial journey. She knows what she wants her money to do because of her very own money reasons. She makes choices that will lead to the life that she wants to create. She does not leave her finances to chance but, rather, makes deliberate and well-thought-out decisions from a place of knowledge because she knows the importance of

RICH HABITS

A financially empowered woman makes choices based on unbiased and current information. She does not leave her wealth management to chance, but rather, makes deliberate and well-thought-out decisions from a place of knowledge. She then monitors the choices she has made, and makes proactive changes as necessary.

doing so. She then monitors the choices she has made and makes proactive changes when necessary. She is confident and assured because she is informed and attentive with her money. She knows this will lead to what she really wants in life. She knows that she can change the lives of others. She knows that it is not about the money; it's about her life and what she chooses to do with it. It's about creating a rich life with how she earns, grows and gives her time, talents and money.

Financial Woman Steps

Review your money reasons daily over your morning coffee, or keep them in your bedside drawer for a quick review.

Look over your Own and Owe statement now that you have completed this book.

What steps from this book will you put in your calendar now?

LINGO AND REFERENCES

401-K – Personal retirement savings account

AICPA – American Institute of Certified Public Accountants

Ben Bernanke – Chairman of the Federal Reserve Board

Bernie Madoff – Bernard Lawrence is a former stock broker, investment advisor, non-executive chairman of the NASDAQ stock market, and the admitted operator of what has been described as the largest Ponzi scheme in history. (Wikipedia)

Cash Flow – The amount of money that flows in and out of a business or household

Craigslist – National and Local job and other classified business listings

CPA – Certified Public Account

elance.com – Job-posting site to hire internet workers for your specific project needs

ETF – Exchange Traded Fund

FDIC – Federal Deposit Insurance Corporation; a defined government corporation which guarantees deposits in member banks

FINRA – Financial Industry Regulatory Authority. FINRA is the largest independent regulator for all securities firms doing business in the United States

Forbes 400 – Forbes Magazine's annual list of the world's 400 richest people in America

guru.com – Job-posting site to hire internet workers for your specific project needs

Index Fund – An A type of Mutual Fund with a portfolio constructed to match or track the components of a market index, such as the Standard & Poor's 500 Index (S&P 500). An index mutual fund is said to provide broad market exposure, low operating expenses and low portfolio turnover. (Investopedia)

IRA – Individual Retirement Account; type of retirement plan with tax advantages

NASDAQ – National Association of Securities Dealers Automated Quotations. The stock exchange which specializes in Tech stocks.

Net Worth – The difference between what you own and what you owe

Profit/Loss or P/L – Profit & Loss

REIT – Real Estate Investment Trust

Roth IRA – Roth Individual Retirement Accounts (IRA) are funded with money which has been taxed already. Regular IRAs are funded with pre-tax dollars and are taxed only when the funds are withdrawn.

SEC – Securities and Exchange Commission

SIPC – Securities Investor Protection Corporation

WEBSITES

**The following free handouts
referenced in this book are available at
http://www.FinancialWoman.com/tools**

Affirmations to inspire you to have a healthy mindset so you can have good money habits and grow your money

Own and Owe Statement "fill in the blank" template to help you know exactly how much money you have so you can move toward creating what you want

Visual Money Flow Chart shows you the significance of positive cash flow in growing your money

Covered Call Writing handout provides information on this common option strategy used to generate income from stocks and etf's

Investment Objective Summary handout clarifies the possible outcomes from each of your investments to help you choose the right type of investment

Investing Basics handout lists everything you'll definitely want to know about any investment you own so you can have control of your money

Financial Professional Credentials handout outlines the various types of credentials and the related requirements of each type so you'll feel more knowledgeable and confident about your choices

Other:

FINRA – Check the history and/or practices of a Broker http://www.finra.org/Investors/ToolsCalculators/ BrokerCheck/

Made in the USA
Charleston, SC
08 November 2011